Meditations for Lent

Also by Jacques-Bénigne Bossuet
from Sophia Institute Press:

Meditations for Advent

Jacques-Bénigne Bossuet

Meditations for Lent

Edited and translated by
Christopher O. Blum

SOPHIA INSTITUTE PRESS
Manchester, New Hampshire

Meditations for Lent is a selection and translation of *Méditations sur l'Évangile*, in *Oeuvres choisies de Bossuet* (Paris: Roger et Chernoviz, no date); *Élévations à Dieu sur tous les mystères de la religion chrétienne*, in *Oeuvres complètes de Bossuet*, edited by Abbé Guillaume (Lyon: Briday, 1879); and *Oeuvres Oratoires de Bossuet*, édition critique de l'abbé J. Lebarq, revue et augmentée par Ch. Urbain et E. Levesque, 7 volumes (Paris: Desclée de Brouwer, 1914-1926).

Sophia Institute Press
Box 5284, Manchester, NH 03108
1-800-888-9344
www.SophiaInstitute.com

Sophia Institute Press® is a registered trademark of Sophia Institute.

Library of Congress Cataloging-in-Publication Data

Bossuet, Jacques Bénigne, 1627-1704.

[Meditations. English]

Meditations for Lent / Jacques-Benigne Bossuet ; edited and translated by Christopher O. Blum.

pages cm

"Meditations for Lent is a selection and translation of Méditations sur L'Evangile, in Oeuvres choisies de Bossuet (Paris: Roger et Chernoviz, no date); élévations à Dieu sur tous les mystères de la religion chrétienne, in Oeuvres complétes de Bossuet, edited by Abbe Guillaume (Lyon: Briday, 1879); and Oeuvres Oratoires de Bossuet, édition critique de l'Abbé J. Lebarq, révue et augmentée par Ch. Urbain et E. Levesque, 7 volumes (Paris: Desclée de Brouwer, 1914-1924)"—E-Cip t.p. verso

ISBN 978-1-933184-99-9 (pbk. : alk. paper) 1. Lent—Meditations. 2. Spiritual life—Catholic Church. I. Blum, Christopher Olaf, 1969- translator. II. Title.

BV85.B64413 2014

242'.34—dc23

2013033857

Contents

Week 1

Week 2

Week 3

Week 4

Week 5

Holy Week

Foreword

"Lord, will those who are saved be few?" (Luke 13:23). Such was the anxious question on the part of someone whose path Jesus had crossed on his way to Jerusalem, to his Passion and death. At what might have been about the same time in the Gospel story, *the most important question* in human history was also asked, although this time by the Lord: "But who do you say that I am?" (Matt. 16:15). And once that question is answered by the Prince of the Apostles — "You are the Christ, the Son of the living God" (Matt. 16:16) — and by each of us in turn, the thoughts in the mind of the sincere inquirer naturally turn to the next great subject: salvation itself.

Jesus did not answer the person's question, at least not as it was posed. Instead, he went straight to the heart of the matter by making the question *personal*, which, of course, it was from the beginning. "Strive to enter by the narrow door," the Lord replied (Luke 13:24). We might understand him this way: "You, you give your heart to me, without reserve; this is the one thing needful. Do not allow your attention or your affections to be drawn away from my words, from my Sacred Heart. I am the Good Shepherd who will never leave you. In love, I will offer my life for you on Calvary; in love, will you offer your life for me and not count the cost? This is the proof of friendship, of love: to give all. I am the door; if you enter by me, you will be saved. You say that I am Lord, the Messiah. Now give this belief flesh in your life. Follow me to Jerusalem."

Lent is the journey of the Mystical Body of Christ to Jerusalem, to the fulfillment of the Paschal Mystery. We wish to accompany Jesus and not simply allow him to cross our path. Our concern for eternal salvation must be urgent, but not "anxious and troubled" (Luke 10:41). We can see the confusion, the neglect, the malice of the world, just as the person who posed the question to the Lord did. Although we are aware of these things and saddened by them, they do not make us fearful or unsteady. The questioner in the Gospel saw the challenge and became fainthearted. But Jesus looked into the eyes of the person and imparted purpose and strength, peace and hope. Appealing to what was noble within, he said, in effect, "Do not be afraid of what you see in a fallen world and in your own human weakness. Walk with me, and let the fire in my heart change yours."

Why look to Jacques-Bénigne Bossuet to help us on our Lenten pilgrimage to Jerusalem with the Good Shepherd? "The whole of the Christian life consists in making this journey [to Heaven] well," he wrote, "and it was to that end that our Lord directed all his deeds." A student of St. Vincent de Paul, Bossuet became famous as an orator in France in the seventeenth century and one who has been compared very favorably with two of the Church's greatest preachers: St. Augustine and St. John Chrysostom, whose theological writings and sermons helped to shape Bossuet's. But most importantly, Bossuet's work reflects his lifelong love for and study of Sacred Scripture and his vital interior life, and as such it has been prized by holy souls such as Blessed Junípero Serra and Pope Pius XII, who kept Bossuet's writing on his bedside table. Bossuet was also a favorite of the influential retreat master of the twentieth century, Fr. Edward Leen.

The meditations here are drawn from the spiritual writings of Bossuet and arranged to accord with the Gospels (and in some cases the Old Testament lessons) of the season of Lent and of the two great solemnities that fall during the Lenten season. They shed light particularly on our need for conversion and mercy and on the importance of forgiving those who trespass against us, so that we in turn might receive God's mercy. As such, they give form to how we must "strive to enter by the narrow door," just as the Master instructed us.

"O Jesus! I present myself to you to make my journey in your company," Bossuet says. "O my Savior, receive your traveler! Here, I am ready, holding on to nothing. I want to leave this world with you and go to the Father."

Fr. Paul Check
November 2013

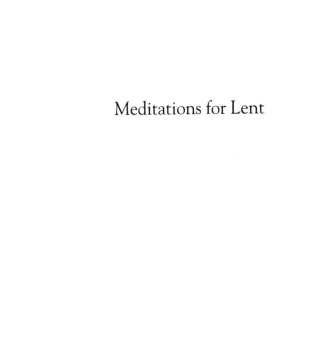

Meditations for Lent

Ash Wednesday

Pray to God in Secret

"Go into your room" (Matt. 6:6) — that is, into the most private part of your home, or rather, go into the most intimate place in your heart. Recollect yourself completely. "Shut the door" (Matt. 6:6). Shut your senses, and let no foreign thoughts enter. "Pray in secret." Open your heart to God alone. Let him be the keeper of your innermost sorrows.

"Do not heap up empty phrases" (Matt. 6:7). It is unnecessary to tell God your needs in lengthy speeches, for he knows all of them before you say a word. Tell him interiorly about what will profit you, and recollect yourself in God. The prayers of the pagans, who do not know God, are only a heap of senseless phrases. Say little with your lips and much in your heart. Do not multiply your thoughts, for doing so will only confuse and tire you. Bring your attention to rest upon some important truth that captures your mind and heart. Consider, weigh, and taste it; ruminate upon it; enjoy it. Truth is the bread of the soul. You do not need to swallow each morsel whole. Nor do you need always to be passing from one truth to another. Hold on to one, embracing it until it becomes a part of you. Attach your heart to it even more than your mind. Draw forth all of its juices by pressing it with your attention.

God sees you in secret. Know that he sees into your very depths, infinitely farther than you do yourself. Make a simple, lively act of faith in his presence. Christian soul, place yourself entirely under his gaze. He is very near. He is present, for he gives being and motion to all things. Yet you must believe more; you must believe with a lively faith that he is present to you by giving you all of your good thoughts from within, as holding in his hand the source from which they come, and not only the good thoughts, but also whatever good desires, good resolutions, and every good act of the will, from its very first beginning and birth to its final perfection. Believe, too, that he is in the souls of the just, and that he makes his dwelling there within, according to these words of the Lord: "We will come to him and make our home with him" (John 14:23). He is there in a stable and permanent way: he makes his home there. Desire that he should be in you in this way. Offer yourself to him as his dwelling and temple.

Now come out, and with the same faith that enables you to see him within you, look upon him in Heaven, where he manifests himself to his beloved. It is there that he awaits you. Run. Fly. Break your chains; break all the bonds that tie you down to flesh and blood. O God, when shall I see you? When will I have that pure heart that enables you to be seen, in yourself, outside of yourself, everywhere? O Light that enlightens the world! O Life that gives life to all the living! O Truth that feeds us all! O Good that satisfies us all! O Love that binds all together! I praise you, my heavenly Father, who sees me in secret.

Our Life, a Journey to God

Let us read the words of St. John. "Before the feast of the Passover, when Jesus knew that his hour had come to depart out of this world to the Father, having loved his own who were in the world, he loved them to the end" (John 13:1).

We know that the word *Passover* signifies a journey. One of the reasons for this name is that the feast of Passover was instituted when the chosen people had to come out of Egypt in order to go to the land that had been promised to their fathers. This was a prefigurement of the journey that the new chosen people would have to make to their home in Heaven. The whole of the Christian life consists in making this journey well, and it was to that end that our Lord directed all of his deeds, as St. John seems to be telling us here.

The first thing that we should notice is that we must make this Passover, this journey, with Jesus Christ. For this reason, the evangelist begins the account of this Passover of our Lord with these words: "Before the feast of Passover, when Jesus knew that his hour had come to depart out of this world to the Father."

O Jesus! I present myself to you to make my journey in your company. I wish to depart from this world with you to your Father, whom you have wished to be my own. "The world passes away," says your apostle (1 John 2:17). "The form of this world is passing away" (1 Cor. 7:31), but I do not wish to pass away with this world; I wish to pass over to your Father. This is the journey that I have to make, and I want to make it with you. In the old Passover, the Jews who were to leave Egypt for the Promised Land had to present themselves in traveler's garb, with staff in hand and loins girt and sandals on their feet, and they had to "eat in haste," ready to march at any moment (Exod. 12:11). This is the image of the condition in which the Christian should place himself in order to make his Passover with Jesus, in order to pass to his Father with him. O my Savior, receive your traveler! Here I am ready, holding on to nothing. I want to leave this world with you and go to the Father.

Why do I hesitate to leave? Am I still attached to this life? What error pins me to this place of exile? You are going to depart, my Savior, and resolved though I am to go with you, yet I am troubled when I am told that all good things must be left behind.

Cowardly traveler: what do you fear? The journey that you have to make is that same one that our Savior will make in our Gospel: are you afraid to go with him? Listen: "Jesus knew that his hour had come to depart out of this world." What is there that is so lovable in this world that you are unwilling to leave it with your Savior Jesus? Would he have left it, if it were good to remain in? Listen, once again, Christian: "Jesus departs out of this world to go to the Father." If it were necessary to leave this world without going to a better place—even if this world be a small thing and we lose little in losing it—we could regret it because we would not have anything better. Yet this is not the kind of journey you must make. Jesus leaves this world to go to his Father. Christian, you depart for a Father. The place you are leaving is one of exile, and you will return to the paternal home.

Let us then depart from this world with joy, but let us not wait until our final moments to begin the journey. When the Israelites went forth from Egypt, they did not immediately arrive in the Promised Land. Although they had forty years still to wander in the desert, they celebrated their Passover because they were leaving Egypt and beginning their journey. Let us learn to celebrate our

Our Life, a Journey to God

Passover from the very first step. Let our journey be a perpetual one. Let us never stop, let us never remain in one place, but let us always make our camp according to the example of the Israelites. May everything be a desert to us, as it was to them. Let us like them always live beneath a tent, for our house is everywhere. Let us march, march, march, and make our journey with Jesus. Let us die to the world daily. Let us say with the apostle, "I die every day" (1 Cor. 15:31). I am not of the world. I am passing through, holding on to nothing.

Friday after Ash Wednesday

God Alone Suffices

"Lord, show us the Father, and we shall be satisfied" (John 14:8). God alone suffices, and all we need to possess him is to see him, because in seeing him, we see all his goodness, as he himself explained to Moses: "I will make all my goodness pass before you" (Ex. 33:19). We see all that attracts our love, and we love him beyond all limits. Let us join St. Philip in saying with all our heart, "Lord, show us the Father, and we shall be satisfied." He alone can fill all our emptiness, satisfy all our needs, content us, and make us happy.

Let us then empty our heart of all other things, for if the Father alone suffices, then we have no need for sensible goods, less for exterior wealth, and still less for the honor of men's good opinion. We do not even need this mortal life; how then can we need those things necessary to preserve it? We need only God. He alone suffices. In possessing him we are content.

God Alone Suffices

How courageous are these words of St. Philip! To say them truthfully, we must also be able to say with the apostles: "Lord, we have left everything and followed you" (cf. Matt. 19:27). At the least we must leave everything by way of affection, desire, and resolution, that is, by an invincible resolution to attach ourselves to nothing, to seek no support except in God alone. Happy are they who carry this desire to its limit, who make the final, lasting, and perfect renunciation! But let them not leave anything for themselves. Let them not say: "This little thing to which I am still attached, it is a mere nothing." We know the nature of the human heart. Whenever a little thing is left to it, there the heart will place all its desires. Strip it all away; break from it; let it go. To own things as though one had nothing, to be married as though one were not, to make use of this world as though one were not using it, but as though it did not exist, and as though we were not a part of it: this is the true good for which we should strive. We are not Christians if we cannot say sincerely with St. Philip, "Show us the Father, and we shall be satisfied."

It is from the very depths of faith that these words are spoken, and it is in a certain sense from the very foundation of nature itself. For in the depths of our nature we sense our need to possess God, that he alone is capable of fulfilling our nature, and that we are anxious and tormented when separated from him. When, therefore, surrounded by other goods, we sense this inevitable void and something tells us that we are unhappy, it is the depth of our nature that, in its way, cries, "Show us the Father, and we shall be satisfied." But what good is the sick man's desire to be well while he lacks every remedy and while death lies within him, without his knowing it? Such is the condition of human nature itself. Man, abandoned to himself, does not know what to do, nor what to become. His pleasures carry him off, and these very same pleasures destroy him. With each sin of the senses he gives himself a killing blow, and he not only kills his soul by his intemperance, in his blindness and ignorance he kills the very body that he would flatter. Since the Fall, man is born to be unhappy. The infirmities of a body in which he places all his good make him so. How much more unhappy is he made by the great mass of errors, lawless deeds, and vicious inclinations that are the maladies and the death of his soul! What a miserable seduction reigns in us! We do not know how to desire or ask for what we need.

St. Philip's words teach us everything. He limits himself to what Jesus taught us is the one thing needful. Lord, you are the way. I come to you to find myself again and to say with your apostle, "Show us the Father, and we shall be satisfied."

Saturday after Ash Wednesday

The Truth and the Life

"I am the truth and the life" (cf. John 14:6). I am the Word that was "at the beginning," the word of the eternal Father, his concept, his wisdom, the true light that enlightens every man (John 1:9). I am the truth itself and consequently the support, the nourishment, and the life of all who hear me, the one in whom there is life, the same life that is in the Father.

It is in and through faith that we must consider these things, for if they were not necessary to our salvation, Jesus would not have revealed them to us.

I am the truth and the life, he says, because I am God; but at the same time I am man. I am come to instruct mankind by bringing the words of eternal life, and together with this teaching I have given the example of how to live well. Yet as all of this remained only an outer work, it was still necessary to bring grace to men, and so I made myself their victim in order to merit this grace for them. Men can approach God and eternal life only through my doctrine, my example, my merits, and the grace that I bring to the world. "For the law was given through Moses; grace and truth came through Jesus Christ ... [and] we have beheld his glory, glory as of the only Son from the Father" (John 1:17, 14). Let us enter by this way, and we will find truth and life.

It is astonishing to think that one could be both means and end together at once, the "truth and life" which are the terminus and at the same time the "way" that is to be traveled. Yet Jesus explains this mystery to us. What can lead us to truth, if not the truth itself? The truth is sovereign. No one can force it or move it in any way; it must give itself to us freely. It is when we possess the truth, that is to say, when we know it, when we love it, when we embrace it that we really live. God forbid that we imagine we have arms to encompass it! We enjoy it as we enjoy the light: by seeing it. The truth convinces all those who see it as it is, for the truth reveals to us everything beautiful and is itself the most beautiful of all the objects that it can reveal to us.

To see light, all we need do is open our eyes; the light comes in by itself. There is no other path that we need to take to light. Now truth is more light than light itself, so nothing can take us to truth other than truth itself. It must approach us, humble itself, and make itself lowly. And what is Jesus if not this very truth which comes toward us, which hides itself under a form that accommodates itself to our weakness, to show itself as much as our weak eyes can stand to see? And so, in order to be the way, he also had to be the truth.

Come then, O Truth! You yourself are my life, and because you come close to me, you are my way. What do I have to fear? How can I be anxious? Do I fear that I will not find the way that leads to truth? The way itself, as St. Augustine said, presents itself to us; the way itself comes to us. Come then and live by the truth, reasonable and intelligent soul! What light there is in the teaching of Jesus!

This light is all the more beautiful for shining amid the darkness. But let us take care lest we be like those of whom it is written: "The light has come into the world, and men loved darkness rather than light, because their deeds were evil" (John 3:19). Of what use to me is a light that reveals only my ugliness and shame? Retire from me, Light; I cannot endure you. Holy doctrine of the Gospel, eternal truth, all-too-faithful mirror: you make me tremble! We cannot change the truth; let us then change ourselves, for we exist only by a ray of the truth that is within us.

Let us love the truth. Let us love Jesus, who is the truth itself. Let us change ourselves so that we may be like him. Let us not put ourselves in a condition that will oblige us to hate the truth. The one who is condemned by the truth hates and flees it. Let there be nothing false in one who is the disciple of the truth. Let us live by the truth and feed ourselves with it. It is for this that the Eucharist is given to us. It is the body of Jesus, his holy humanity, the pure grain that nourishes the elect, the pure substance of truth, the bread of life, and it is at the same time the way, the truth, and the life. If Jesus Christ is our way, let us not walk in the ways of the world. Let us enter into the narrow gate through which he walked. Above all, let us be mild and humble. Man's falsehood is his pride, because in truth he is nothing, and God alone *is*. This is the pure and only truth.

Tempted in the Desert

Jesus, "full of the Holy Spirit" who had settled upon him under the figure of a dove, "returned from the Jordan, and was led by the Spirit" into the desert (Luke 4:1). Immediately after his baptism, full of the spirit of groaning (cf. Rom. 8:23), Jesus, that innocent dove, went to fast and weep for our sins in solitude. According to St. Matthew, he was "led up by the Spirit" (Matt. 4.1); according to St. Mark, the Spirit "drove him" (Mark 1:12). Whichever be the case, we see that by baptism we are separated from the world and consecrated to fasting and abstinence and to the battle against temptation. This is what happened to the Savior of the world as soon as he had been baptized.

Christian life is a retreat. We are "not of the world," just as Jesus Christ is "not of the world" (John 17:14). What is the world? It is, as St. John said, the "lust of the flesh," that is, sensuality and corruption in our desires and deeds; "the lust of the eyes," curiosity, avarice, illusion, fascination, error, and folly in the affectation of learning; and, finally, pride and ambition (1 John 2:16). To these evils of which the world is full, and which make up its substance, a retreat must be set in opposition. We need to make ourselves into a desert by a holy detachment.

Christian life is a battle. The demon from whom a soul escapes "brings with him seven other spirits more evil than himself" (Matt. 12:45) in order to tempt us anew. We must never cease to fight. In this battle, St. Paul teaches us to make an eternal abstinence, that is, to cut ourselves off from the pleasures of the senses and guard our hearts from them. "Every athlete exercises self-control in all things. They do it to receive a perishable wreath, but we an imperishable" (1 Cor. 9:25).

It was to repair and to expiate the failings of our retreat, of our battle against temptations, of our abstinence, that Jesus was driven into the desert. His fast of forty days prefigured the lifelong one that we are to practice by abstaining from evil deeds and by containing our desires within the limits laid down by the law of God. This should be the first effect of Jesus' fast. If he calls us higher and draws us not only to a renunciation of the heart, but to an actual departure from the world, happy shall we be to go and fast with Jesus Christ: let us find our happiness in the desert with him!

Tempted in the Desert

"And he was in the desert," St. Mark tells us, "forty days, tempted by Satan; and he was with the wild beasts; and the angels ministered to him" (cf. Mark 1:13). Here we see, as if in a painting, Jesus alone in the desert, where the Devil is his tempter, the beasts his company, and the angels his ministers.

Why is Jesus with the beasts? Why does he give himself such companions in the desert? "Flee men," said a voice to a hermit of old. The beasts have remained in their natural condition, and, so to speak, in their innocence, while among men everything has been perverted by sin. "All flesh had corrupted their way upon the earth" (Gen. 6:12). In the society of men we find dissimulation, infidelity, self-interested friendship, a mutually interested exchange of flattery, lies, secret envy joined with showy but false benevolence, inconstancy, injustice, and corruption. Let us flee all this, at least in spirit; it will be better to live with beasts than with men of the world.

We will be exposed to temptation with Jesus, but like him we will have angels to minister to us. They came to serve the Savior in his hour of need, in the weakened condition that he chose to be in at the end of his long fast. Yet we should also remember that they are "ministering spirits sent forth to serve, for the sake of those who are to obtain salvation" (Heb. 1:14), and that in honor of the

Savior they make themselves the ministers of those who fast with him in the desert, who love prayer and retirement, and who live abstaining from what brings contentment to nature, never giving their hearts over to it.

I Was Hungry and You Fed Me

Lord Jesus, my life and my hope, I place myself in your holy presence, to see and to consider in your light, in faith and in perpetual recognition of your goodness, how you yourself bore our misery and infirmity to the point of being able to say, "I was hungry, I was thirsty, I was naked, a prisoner, sick," in the person of all those who have had to suffer such woes.

What brought you to bear our burdens, O Jesus, was the love that led you to take on our nature, and not to take it on immortal and healthy, as you had originally made it, but to take it on as sin and your justice had made it—mortal, infirm, and poor—because you wished to carry our sin. You wished to bear our sin on the Cross as an innocent victim, and you wished to bear it throughout your life, the "Lamb who takes away the sin of the world" (cf. John 1:29). You took away our sin by carrying it yourself. But you are the Holy of holies, "anointed with the oil of gladness above your fellows" (cf. Ps. 45:7) and bearing the name of Christ. This oil by which you are anointed and sanctified is the divinity that is united to your holy soul and unstained body. Being the true Holy One of God and thus unable join us in our iniquity or the stain of our sin, you carried only its just punishment, that is, our mortality and all that follows from it. In this way you became sensible to our woes, a compassionate high priest who had experienced them himself. For, as your apostle said, "He had to be made like his brethren in every respect, so that he might become a merciful and faithful high priest in the service of God, to make expiation for the sins of the people" (Heb. 2:17).

May you be forever praised, O great High Priest, for you have taken pity on our suffering, and not as the happy have pity on those who suffer, but as the unhappy have pity on one another, through the understanding of their common misery. For it was your pleasure to be reckoned among those the world calls wretched and to be seen as one with "no form or comeliness," to be "despised and rejected by men," in a word, "a man of sorrows, and acquainted with grief" (Isa. 53:2-3). Having experienced all of the suffering that attends our sinful nature, you are "able to sympathize with our weaknesses" (cf. Heb. 4:15). Although you did not suffer any of the particular illnesses by which we are so frequently put on trial, you bore hunger, thirst, weakness, and all the other common maladies of our nature. You also bore anxiety, fear, danger, and distress: the most terrible of our woes. And you bore wounds that cut your holy body into pieces.

You have yourself felt the greatest, the most terrifying, and the most sorrowful infirmities to which our poor human nature is heir. This is why you have compassion upon all our woes, even including our illnesses, and you never cured the sick or raised the dead or healed the infirm without first being moved by pity. Thus you cried before you raised Lazarus. Thus you multiplied the loaves for the people who were "harassed and helpless" (Matt. 9:36). And on a similar occasion you said, "I have compassion on the crowd, because they have been with me now three days, and have nothing to eat; and I am unwilling to send them away hungry, lest they faint on the way" (Matt. 15:32). The blind men, who knew how sensible you were of their suffering, cried aloud to you, "Have mercy on us, Son of David!" You heard their voices and, touched by compassion, placed your merciful hand upon their lightless eyes, and they received their sight (Matt. 20:30-34). And you wept over the coming woes of Jerusalem (Luke 19:41). It was this tender and compassionate heart, this heart moved by pity, that solicited your all-powerful arm in favor of those whose sufferings you saw. In this way, your compassion was the source of your miracles, which is what led your evangelist to write that you "took our infirmities and bore our diseases" (Matt. 8:17). You truly bore them in your compassion, and you comforted your own heart by healing them.

O my Savior, you bore these sentiments of compassion to Heaven, and although you were not able to carry the tears, the groaning, and the interior sufferings that you felt in the face of all of the evils with which our nature is burdened, you have borne the memory of them there, a memory which makes you tender, merciful, and compassionate toward all of your members, toward all those who suffer on earth. For you are that charitable Samaritan (Luke 10:33) who takes pity on all who are injured, from whatever nation they come. Thus do I feel, my Lord, the truth of these words: "I was hungry, I was thirsty, I was injured" in all those who have been afflicted by these woes.

Take away from me, O my Savior, this heart of stone. Let me be as compassionate as you. Let me say with your apostle: "Who is weak, and I am not weak? Who is made to fall, and I am not indignant?" (2 Cor. 11:29). Let me rejoice, according to his precept, with "those who rejoice," which is easy and agreeable to nature, but let me weep sincerely "with those who weep" (Rom. 12:15). Let me be able to say with you, "I am hungry, I thirst, I am a foreigner without lodging, I am a prisoner, I am sick" with all those who are thus afflicted. Let my compassion not be in vain; let it lead me to help them. May I ease their burdens as effectively as if I were seeking to help myself. Let me see still further: let me continually remember that you carried their infirmities in yourself, that you suffer in all of them, finally, that you will repeat at the Last Judgment "as you did it to the least of these my brethren"—for you will not disdain any sort of lowliness—"you did it to me" (cf. Matt. 25:40).

To you be the glory and praise and thanksgiving of all those who suffer, that is to say, of all men whatever, for your goodness in taking up their sufferings and making them your own and recommending them to all your children by a precept which is the only one that you will speak from your throne, before Heaven and earth, in the presence of men and angels. Amen. Amen.

Our Father

From the very first word of the Lord's Prayer, our hearts melt with love. God wants to be our father by adopting us, one by one. He has an only-begotten Son in whom he delights. Sinners he adopts. Men adopt children when they have none of their own. God, having such a Son, has nevertheless adopted us. Adoption is a work of love, because we choose the one whom we adopt. Nature gives other children; love alone makes adoptive ones. God, who loves his only-begotten Son with all his love, even unto infinity, extends the love he has for his Son to us. That is what Jesus said in the admirable prayer that he made to his Father for us: "that the love with which you have loved me may be in them, and I in them" (John 17:26). Let us then love such a Father. Let us say a thousand times: Our Father, our Father, our Father, will I not love you always? Will we not always be true children enfolded in your paternal tenderness?

Our Father

What is it that makes us say Our Father? Let us learn from St. Paul: "because you are sons, God has sent the Spirit of his Son into our hearts, crying, 'Abba! Father!'" (Gal. 4:6). It is the Holy Spirit in us. It is the Spirit who forms in us our heart's invocation of God as a Father always ready to hear us. The same St. Paul says elsewhere: "All who are led by the Spirit of God are sons of God," and that God sends us "the spirit of sonship" by which we cry "Abba! Father!" (Rom. 8:14-15). Once again, it is the Holy Spirit who gives us this filial cry.

Why should it be called a cry? We cry when in great need. A child cries only when it suffers or when it has a need. To whom does the child cry in his need if not to his father, his mother, his nursemaid, to all those in whose nature he senses something paternal? Let us cry then, for our needs are extreme. We are falling, seduced by sin, carried away by the pleasures of the senses. Let us cry—we cannot do more—but let us cry to our Father. The Holy Spirit, the God who is Love, the love of the Father and of the Son, the one by whom "God's love has been poured into our hearts," will lead us (Rom. 5:5). Let us cry ardently, and let all our bones cry out: O God, you are our Father!

"It is the Spirit," St. Paul adds, "bearing witness with our spirit that we are children of God" (Rom. 8:16).

O God, who is it that hears this testimony of the Holy Spirit, who tells us interiorly that we are children of God? When we enjoy the peace of a good conscience and of a heart that has nothing for which to reproach itself that would separate it from God, there is a voice that says secretly to us in the intimate silence of our heart: God is your Father, and you are his son! Alas, this voice is too intimate, and too few people hear it. Let it speak again, and we will understand it better. We must be made stronger and better rooted in the good. The Holy Spirit does not give everyone this secret testimony. As to him, he wishes to give it to all, but all are not worthy. O God, make us worthy of it! This is a good thing to ask of God, for in truth it is he who gives it. And he responds: Act with me, work by my side, open your heart to me, let every created thing be silent, and say to me often in secret: Our Father, our Father.

Week 1: Wednesday

The Sign of Jonah

Jonah did not want to go to the Ninevites and preach doom. He feared that if God were to pardon them—as in his immense goodness he was wont to do—the pagans would be confirmed in their unbelief and would have contempt for the Lord's threats and for the words of his prophets.

Impelled by the prophetic spirit, which was pressing upon him internally, Jonah said to God: Lord, this is a message that I cannot deliver, for I know that "you are a gracious God and merciful, slow to anger and abounding in mercy, and that you repent of evil" and are always ready to forgive men their iniquities (Jonah 4:2). You will once again pardon this unbelieving city. They will no longer listen to those who speak in your name. In vain will we make known the rigor of your judgments to Judah and Israel. Your ease and indulgence will harden men in their evil. O Lord, said Jonah, take my life, for "it is better for me to die" (Jonah 4:8) than to be found a lying prophet and to expose prophecy to derision.

In his extreme distress, not only did Jonah seek to avoid hearing the prophecy, but he fled from the Lord, taking ship at Joppa to go to the other end of the world. We must not persuade ourselves that the holy prophet believed that he could pass out of God's sight or leave God's empire by traveling to a far-off land. After all, we will soon hear him say to the mariners, "I am a Hebrew; and I fear the Lord, the God of heaven, who made the sea and the dry land" (Jonah 1:9). Jonah knew full well that it was impossible to escape God's power or to leave his kingdom. The face of God that he was attempting to flee, this presence that he wished to avoid, was the face that God shows interiorly to his prophets. This is the presence by which he enlightens their spirit when he sees fit to inspire them. This was the face that Jonah believed he could escape by separating himself from the Holy Land and from the people of Israel, where God had been accustomed to pour forth prophecy.

He fled, therefore, both the Holy Land and Nineveh at once, not believing that God would want to bring him back against his will. But he had no sooner gone on board when "the Lord hurled a great wind upon the sea, and there was a mighty tempest on the sea, so that the ship threatened to break up." While "each cried to his god" with horrible wailing, and they "threw the wares that were in the ship into the sea to lighten the load," Jonah, without wondering at his great peril—for we often see that those strong souls who are under the hand of God fear nothing but him alone—went "down to the inner part of the ship and had lain down, and was fast asleep" (cf. Jonah 1:4-5). In this he was like Jesus, who, in a similar storm, slept peacefully on a cushion and allowed the waves to fill the boat in which he was with his disciples (Mark 4:37-38). By a similar mystery, and to show that we have nothing to fear when God is with us, and that all we can do in any event is to abandon ourselves to his will, Jonah slept amid the wailing and the terrible clamor of the wind and waves until he was awakened—in just about the same manner the Savior was—when they said to him, "What do you mean, you sleeper? Arise, call upon your god! Perhaps the god will give a thought to us, that we do not perish" (Jonah 1:6).

The hand of God never left his holy prophet. Jonah immediately sensed that the storm had been sent against him. Calmly he watched the passengers cast lots to discover the cause of the storm. He saw the lot fall on himself without fear, for he preferred to die than to prophesy, be contradicted, and see prophecy blasphemed (Jonah 4:3).

He spoke boldly to the mariners, who wished to spare him: "Throw me into the sea" without delay, "then the sea will quiet down for you; for I know it is because of me that this great tempest has come upon you" (Jonah 1:12). Astonished by his extraordinary calm, they respected him and, even more, the greatness of the God he served. They made their utmost effort to regain land without it costing his life. But the more they rowed, the more the sea rose, until they were constrained to throw Jonah into the sea, taking God as their witness that they drowned him only with regret and were innocent of his death. Immediately, the "sea ceased from its raging" (1:15). And here already, in prefigurement of our Savior, all the people were saved from death—as they believed—by the holy prophet, who had voluntarily offered himself for them. Yet this is not the whole of the mystery. The rest is explained by the Savior himself: "An evil and adulterous generation seeks for a sign; but no sign shall be given to it except the sign of the prophet Jonah. For as Jonah was three days and three nights in the belly of the whale, so will the Son of man be three days and three nights in the heart of the earth" (Matt. 12:39-40).

The spirit of prophecy did not abandon Jonah in the belly of that enormous fish, for he sang this divine canticle: "Out of the belly of Sheol I cried, and you heard my voice. The waters closed in over me, the deep was round about me ... yet you brought up my life from the Pit, O Lord my God" (Jonah 2:2, 5-6). "And the Lord spoke to the fish, and it vomited out Jonah upon the dry land" (2:10), as a prefigurement of our Savior.

It did not belong to Jonah — who was only the prefigurement — to have all of the characteristics of the truth, nor to have that liberty with respect to death that was reserved to the Savior alone, nor to predict his own death and resurrection. But there is hardly anything that better resembles death and the tomb than the belly of that fish, nor is there a more vivid image of a true and perfect resurrection than the deliverance of Jonah. Let us then adore the one who left "not an iota, not a dot" (Matt. 5:18) of either the prophets or the Law unaccomplished. Let us learn never to lose hope, no matter into what abyss of troubles we are cast, for Jonah came out of the belly of the whale, and Jesus Christ from the tomb and from hell, thus assuring his faithful ones of their own deliverance.

Knock

Ask, seek, knock (Matt.7:7). These are the three degrees and, as it were, the three pleas that must be made with perseverance, blow upon blow. But what must we ask of God in order to emerge from this worse-than-bestial condition in which sin has placed us? We must learn from these words of St. James: "If any of you lacks wisdom, let him ask God, who gives to all men generously and without reproaching … but let him ask in faith, with no doubting" (James 1:5-6).

This is what our Lord himself teaches us: "Truly, I say to you, if you have faith and never doubt … even if you say to this mountain, 'Be taken up and cast into the sea,' it will be done. And whatever you ask in prayer, you will receive, if you have faith" (Matt. 21:21-22).

Consider then where your sin has brought you, and ask with faith for your conversion. Even if the weight of your sins be as great as a mountain, pray and your sins will retreat before your prayer. "Whatever you ask in prayer, if you have faith and never doubt, you will receive." Jesus purposefully made use of this extraordinary comparison to show that everything is possible to the one who prays. So take heart, and do not ever despair of your salvation.

Knock. Persevere in knocking, even to the point of rudeness, if that were possible. There is a way of forcing God and wresting his graces from him, and that way is to ask continually with a firm faith. We must think, with the Gospel: "Ask, and it will be given you; seek, and you will find; knock, and it will be opened to you," which he then repeats by saying, "Every one who asks receives, and he who seeks finds, and to him who knocks it will be opened" (Luke 11:9-10). We must, therefore, pray during the day, pray at night, and pray every time we rise. Even though God seems either not to hear us or even to reject us, we must continually knock, expecting all things from God but nevertheless also acting ourselves. We must not only ask as though God must do everything himself; we must also make our own effort to act according to his will and with the help of his grace, as all things are done with this support. We must never forget that it is always God who provides; to think thus is the very foundation of humility.

"And he told them a parable, to the effect that they ought always to pray and not lose heart" (Luke 18:1).

This perpetual prayer does not consist in a perpetual tension of the mind, which will merely expend all our strength without bringing us to our goal. This perpetual prayer is accomplished when, having prayed the Divine Office, we glean from our prayer and reading some truth or some word that we keep in our heart and that we effortlessly recall from time to time, while holding ourselves as much as possible in a state of dependence toward God and showing our needs to him, that is to say, placing them before his eyes without saying anything. Just as the drought-stricken land seems to call out for rain merely by exposing its dryness to the sky, so also does our soul when we place our needs before God. This is what David said: "My soul thirsts for you like a parched land" (Ps. 143:6).

Lord, I do not need to pray to you; my need itself prays. My neediness prays. My necessity prays. As long as this disposition lasts, we pray without praying. As long as we take care to avoid what would imperil us, we pray without praying, and God understands this language. O Lord, before whom I am, before whom all my misery appears, have pity on it, and all the times that it appears to you, O God most good, let it beg your mercies for me. This is one of the ways of praying always, and, of them, perhaps the most effective.

Week 1: Friday

Christian Righteousness

At the beginning of his explanation of the precepts of the Christian life, Jesus laid as their foundation this beautiful rule: that Christian righteousness must "exceed" that of the most perfect of the Jews and the doctors of the Law (Matt. 5:20). Let us take special care correctly to understand the perfection of the new law of the Gospel, which from our baptism we have sworn to keep.

In order to oblige us to keep his law, Jesus took care to elevate the perfection of Christian righteousness by three degrees. First, we must surpass the wisest of the pagans. This is why he said, "Do not even the Gentiles do the same?" (Matt. 5:47). By this he meant: you should therefore do more. We are told to disdain riches; did not the wise pagans do as much? To be faithful to our friends; were not the pagans as well? To avoid fraud and deceit; did not the pagans detest them? To flee adultery; were not even the most licentious pagans horrified by it?

The second degree is to rise above the justice of the law and of those who know God. And this again in three degrees, by avoiding the three defects of Jewish righteousness. The first is that it was only an exterior righteousness: "Woe to you, scribes and Pharisees, hypocrites! for you cleanse the outside of the cup," which is why you are called "whitewashed tombs" (Matt. 23:25, 27). See the Pharisee in St. Luke: "I am not like other men." And how do you surpass them? "I fast twice a week, I give tithes of all that I get" (Luke 18:11-12). He boasts only about the exterior. Those Christians who are attached only to exterior observances resemble him. To say one's breviary, to go to church, to attend Mass and Vespers, to take holy water, to kneel: in absence of right intention this is a pharisaical righteousness. It seems to be exacting in a certain way, but gains a just reproach from Jesus: "This people honors me with their lips, but their heart is far from me" (Matt. 15:8). It is a false righteousness. But what shall we say about those who do not have even this exterior precision, unless that they are worse than the Pharisees?

The second defect of Jewish righteousness is, as St. Paul says, "being ignorant of the righteousness that comes from God, and seeking to establish their own, they did not submit to God's righteousness" (Rom. 10:3). They thought themselves capable of doing good works by themselves instead of recognizing that it is God who works in them. St. Paul once had this righteousness, but consider how he speaks of it: "as to righteousness under the law, blameless." Note the word *blameless*: it seems as though perfection can be carried to no higher point, and yet he immediately adds: "But whatever gain I had, I counted as loss for the sake of Christ. Indeed I count everything as loss because of the surpassing worth of knowing Christ Jesus my Lord. For his sake I have suffered the loss of all things, and count them as refuse, in order that I may gain Christ and be found in him, not having a righteousness of my own, based on law, but that which is through faith in Christ, the righteousness from God that depends on faith" (cf. Phil. 3:6-9). Here then is the second defect of Jewish righteousness: believing that a man's own works make him righteous. This righteousness is impure and, according to St. Paul, is nothing but refuse because it is nothing but pride. Let us then take care to avoid it, referring humbly to God what little good we accomplish.

But the third defect of Jewish righteousness is that its works fell short in comparison to the standard to which man is held by the Gospel. For by it we are obliged to a greater perfection than those who merely do good. Why? "Because of the surpassing worth of knowing Christ Jesus," as St. Paul said, which is one of the truths that Jesus intended by the words "unless your righteousness exceeds that of the scribes and Pharisees" (Matt. 5:20).

Yet here is something still more excellent, the third degree of perfection, which is that Christian righteousness must rise above itself. "No, brethren," said St. Paul (Phil. 3:12-14), I do not think "that I have already obtained this or am already perfect; but I press on," like a man who does not think that he has yet attained what he desires. "But one thing," but all that I do, all that I seek, all that I think, "forgetting what lies behind"—you see, all of the progress that he has made is nothing to him; he neither stops nor rests—"and straining forward to what lies ahead." Understand this word: he strains, he makes an effort, he goes beyond himself, he suffers a sort of dislocation by the effort that he makes to advance.

Here then is the true Christian, the man who is truly righteous. He believes himself to have done nothing, for if he believed himself to be sufficiently just, then he would not be just at all. We must always advance. "You must be perfect, as your heavenly Father is perfect" (cf. Matt. 5:48). Let us at least desire to be, for to wish to rest in what one has, as if one were assured it would be sufficient, is to renounce righteousness. What is more, if you do not advance, you will falter. For you will be one who "looks back," contrary to the precept of the Gospel. And what will the Savior then decide? That you are not "fit for the kingdom of God" (Luke 9:62).

This is why he said that we must "hunger and thirst for righteousness" (Matt. 5:6). This is no ordinary desire. It is a desire like the one that leads us to eat and to live; it is an ardent and invincible desire that should be kept forever aflame. Whatever your condition, you should have this hunger and thirst; as the capacity of your interior is infinite, so also is the righteousness you seek.

Love Your Enemies

Jesus often spoke about the obligation of fraternal charity. He took us beyond the prohibition of killing or even striking a brother. He said that we must not become angry with our brother, nor show our bitterness toward him by injuring him in any way.

If we have a dispute, we must be easily reconciled, must not seek to bring our disagreement to an end by taking it before a judge, nor even seek a mediator to heal our division. For Christ is the mediator of our reconciliation, and it is the spirit of his charity and grace that should animate us. We ought to be willing to bend, so that, together with our brother, we can be mutually accommodating.

He said that if we come to sense some bitterness in our brother's heart, we must take care to appease him and to prefer reconciliation to sacrifice. But he pushes the obligation still further and uproots the spirit of vengeance. "An eye for an eye and a tooth for a tooth" (cf. Exod.

21:24). This is what was permitted of old, and it seems to be a certain kind of justice. But Jesus does not allow a Christian either to do it himself or to seek satisfaction in this way. If the public authority punishes crimes, the Christian does not prevent it; he respects public order. But for his part, far from avenging himself upon the one who strikes him, he turns the other cheek; he would rather give his coat to the one who would steal his shirt than to seek legal redress for such a small matter and thus burden his mind with legalism and resentment (Matt. 5:39-40). He will more willingly walk two miles with someone who would force him to walk one than seek justice for himself or even dream of causing harm to one who had hurt him. The tranquillity of his heart is more dear to him than the possession of anything that injustice could take away, and if a breach of charity were required to recover something that had been taken away from him, he would not want it at any price.

O gospel, how pure you are! O teaching of Christ, how worthy of our love you are! Yet alas, how poorly we Christians respond to it, and how little worthy are we of so lovely a name!

"Give to him who begs from you, and do not refuse" —as is so often done—"him who would borrow from you" (Matt. 5:42). Do what you can to care for those who suffer: be liberal and beneficent. The sum of the world's riches does not equal the price of these two virtues, nor the reward that they will gain us.

Here then are the three degrees of charity toward our enemies: to love them, to do good to them, and to pray for them. The first is the source of the second: if we love, we give. The last is the one that we think is the easiest to do, but is in fact the most difficult, because it is the one that we must do in relation to God. Nothing should be more sincere, nothing more heartfelt, nothing truer than what we present to the one who sees all, even into the depths of our heart.

Let us examine these three degrees: to love, to do good, and to pray. What is it to "love those who love you"? "Do not even the tax collectors do the same?... Do not even the Gentiles do the same?" (Matt. 5:46-47). It is not for nothing that you are offered an eternal inheritance and an unchanging happiness: it is not to leave you indifferent, or worse than pagans.

Week 2: Sunday

This Is My Beloved Son

The first thing that the eternal Father requires of us when he commands us to listen to his Son is that we be convinced that with regard to all the truths necessary for our salvation, we must refer them to what he said and believe them on his word without further examination. This is the immutable foundation of the entire Christian life. To understand this truth, let us begin by observing that men can come to the truth in two ways: either by their own lights, when they discover it themselves, or by being led by another, as when they believe in a trustworthy report. The distinction is well known, but what follows from it is most admirable.

It belongs to God alone to lead us to the truth by either of these ways. No, men cannot do so, and it is folly to expect them to. The one who undertakes to teach us must either make us understand the truth or at least make us believe it. To make us understand it, much wisdom is necessary; to make us believe it, much authority. Neither readily appears among men. This is why Tertullian said that "the prudence of men is too imperfect to reveal the true good to our reason, and their authority is too weak to be able to require anything from our belief." As a result, we ought to conclude that we should not expect to gain certain knowledge of the truth from men, because their authority is not great enough to make us believe what they say, and their wisdom is too limited to give us understanding.

Yet what we do not find in men is easy to find in God. We will understand this truth if we attentively consider how he speaks in different ways in the Scriptures. Sometimes he makes himself known manifestly, and in such times he says to his people: "You shall know that I am the Lord" (Ezek. 6:7). Sometimes, without revealing himself, he causes his authority to be respected, wishing us to believe him upon his word, as when he says emphatically, so that the whole world is obliged to submit: "Thus says the Lord" and "it will be thus, for I have spoken" (cf. Jer. 34:5). Why this difference? It is because he wishes us to understand that he has the means to make himself heard, but that he has the right to make himself believed. By his infinite light, he can show us his truth openly when it pleases him to do so. And by his sovereign authority, he can oblige us to revere it without our having a full understanding of it. Both are worthy of him. It is worthy of his greatness to rule over our minds either by captivating them by faith or by fulfilling them with a clear vision. The obscurity of faith and the clarity of sight are nevertheless incompatible. What has he then done? Here is the mystery of Christianity. He has divided these two means of teaching between the present and the future life: sight in our heavenly home, faith and submission during the journey. One day, the truth will be revealed. While we wait, to prepare ourselves for it, we must revere authority. Faith will gain the merit; sight is reserved for the reward. There, "as we have heard, so have we seen" (Ps. 48:8). Here, sight is not spoken of; we are only commanded to lend our ears and be attentive to his word: "listen to him" (Luke 9:35).

Let us, therefore, come to Mount Tabor and together run to this divine Master, who shows us the heavenly Father. We can recognize his authority by considering the respect paid to him by Moses and Elijah, that is to say, by the Law and the prophets.

Let us also note that at the same time the voice of the eternal Father commanded us to listen to his Son, Moses and Elijah disappeared and Jesus remained alone. What is this mystery? Why did Moses and Elijah retire at this word? Here is the mystery explained by the great apostle: "In many and various ways God spoke of old to our fathers by the prophets" (Heb. 1:1). Let us hear and understand these words: you have spoken, O Prophets, but you spoke of old, while "in these last days he has spoken to us by a Son" (Heb. 1:2). This is why when Jesus Christ appears as Master, Moses and Elijah retire. The Law, although indeed imperious, makes way for him. The prophets, clairvoyant though they were, nevertheless hide themselves in the cloud (Luke 9:34; Matt. 17:5), as if to say: we spoke of old in the name of and by the order of your Father, but now that you explain the secrets of Heaven yourself, our commission has expired and our authority is incorporated into your superior authority. Being only servants, we humbly cede place to the word of your Son.

Let us, therefore, be attentive and listen to this beloved Son. Let us not search for the reasons for the truths that he teaches us: the sufficient reason is that he has spoken.

Week 2: Monday

And You Will Be Forgiven

There is good reason to be astonished that men should sin so boldly in the sight of Heaven and earth and show so little fear of the most high God. Yet it is a much greater cause of astonishment that while we multiply our iniquities beyond the sands of the sea and have so great a need for God to be kind and indulgent, we are nevertheless so demanding ourselves. Such indignity and such injustice! We want God to suffer everything from us, and we are not able to suffer anything from anyone. We exaggerate beyond measure the faults committed against us; worms that we are, we take the slightest pressure exerted on us to be an enormous attack. Meanwhile, we count as nothing what we undertake proudly against the sovereign majesty of God and the rights of his empire!

Blind and wretched mortals: will we always be so sensitive and delicate? Will we never open our eyes to the truth? Will we never understand that the one who does injury to us is always much more to be pitied than are we who receive the injury? That he pierces his own heart while merely grazing our skin, and that, in the end, our enemies are mad; wanting to make us drink all the venom of their hatred, they do so first themselves, swallowing the very poison they have prepared? Since those who do evil to us are unhealthy in mind, why do we embitter them by our cruel vengeance? Why do we not rather seek to bring them back to reason by our patience and mildness?

Yet we are far removed from these charitable dispositions. Far from making the effort at self-command that would enable us to endure an injury, we think that we are lowering ourselves if we do not take pride in being delicate in points of honor. We even think well of ourselves for our extreme sensitivity. And we carry our resentment beyond all measure, either exercising a pitiless vengeance upon those who anger us, or consoling ourselves with burdening them by making a show of our patience or by feigning tranquillity in order to insult them all the more. We are such cruel enemies and implacable avengers that we even turn patience and pity into the weapons of our anger! Yet these are not our worst excesses, for we do not always wait for actual injuries in order to be irritated. Shadows, jealousies, and hidden opposition suffice to arm us against one another. We often come to hate for the sole reason of believing ourselves to be hated. Anxiety seizes us. We fear injuries before they come, and, carried off by our suspicions, we avenge what has not yet taken place.

All this we must stop. We must take care how we speak about our neighbor. That little word, the dart casually tossed, the malicious tale that gives rise to so many straying thoughts by its affected obliqueness: none of these will fall to the earth. "No secret word is without result" (Wisd. 1:11). We must take care of what we say and bridle our malicious anger and unruly tongues. For there is a God in Heaven who has told us that he will demand a reckoning of our "careless words" (Matt. 12:36): what recompense shall he exact for those which are harmful and malicious? We ought, therefore, to revere his eyes and his presence. Let us ponder the fact that he will judge us as we have judged our neighbor. If we pardon, he will pardon us; if we avenge our injuries, we will "suffer vengeance from the Lord" (Sir. 28:1). His vengeance will pursue us in life and in death, and we will have no rest either in this world or the next.

Let us, then, not wait until the hour of death to pardon our enemies, but let us practice what St. Paul taught: "Do not let the sun go down on your anger" (Eph. 4:26). The apostle's tender, paternal heart could not comprehend that a Christian — a child of peace — could sleep peacefully with a heart that was ulcerated and embittered toward his brother, nor that he could enjoy any rest while willing evil to his neighbor, whose interests God has taken in hand. The light is waning, the sun sets: the apostle gives you no time to waste. You have barely enough time to obey him. We must no longer delay this necessary work. Let us hasten to hand our resentment over to God. If we reserve all of the business of our salvation until the day of our death, it will be far too busy a day. Let us begin now to prepare for the graces that we will need then, and, by pardoning those who hurt us, let us assure ourselves of the eternal mercy of the Father, and of the Son, and of the Holy Spirit. Amen.

Sound No Trumpet

Having lifted Christian righteousness to the utmost perfection — even to the point of giving us God himself for our model — Jesus sees that man, inclined to vanity, will desire to glory in the exterior practices of this perfect righteousness, which is why he gives us this precept: "Beware of practicing your piety before men in order to be seen by them" (Matt. 6:1). He does not prohibit the practice of Christian righteousness in our every encounter, so that our neighbor may be edified by the example. On the contrary, he said: "Let your light so shine before men, that they may see your good works and give glory to your Father who is in heaven" (Matt. 5:16). Yet we must take care not to do them "in order to be seen" by men, for then we will "have no reward" (Matt. 6:1). If you ask for glory from the men and women for whom you work, you should not expect from God anything but the punishment reserved for hypocrites.

Every time you are praised, you should fear these words of the Lord: "Truly, I say to you, they have their reward" (Matt. 6:2). This teaching is so important that Jesus repeats it with each new subject in the same chapter: "Your Father who sees in secret will reward you" (Matt. 6:18).

Remember what he said of the bad rich man: that he received his good things in his lifetime (Luke 16:25). Remember, too, his warning about feasts: "Do not invite your friends or your brothers or your kinsmen or rich neighbors, lest they also invite you in return, and you be repaid" (Luke 14:12).

Happy, then, are they whose "life is hidden with Christ in God" (Col. 3:3), whom the world does not know, who live in the secret of God, contenting themselves with his regard, for what error and folly it is not to be content with such a spectator! They are "as unknown" (2 Cor. 6:9), St. Paul says, for they are not the subjects of the vain speeches of men. "Yet well known" they are (2 Cor. 6:9), for God looks upon them much more than any person so much as thinks of them. Happy, happy are they! "If I were still pleasing men," said the same apostle, "I should not be a servant of Christ" (Gal. 1:10).

We must, however, guard against a nonchalance that would lead us to neglect the exterior actions that edify our neighbor—as if saying, "What is it to me what he thinks?" were equivalent to "What is it to me if he is scandalized?" God forbid! In our exterior actions, we should edify our neighbor. All that we do should be well ordered, down to the very blinking of our eyes. Yet we ought to do everything naturally and without affectation, and we must let the glory be God's.

Be on guard, too, lest you content yourself with exterior order alone: for God is also owed something to look upon in secret, which is a heart that seeks him.

"Do not let your left hand know what your right hand is doing" (Matt. 6:3). Hide your almsgiving from your most intimate friends, and, if possible, do not let the poor themselves know you.

It would be best if you could even hide from yourself the good that you do. At least hide its merit from your eyes. Always believe that you do little, that you do nothing, that you are a useless servant. Always fear that your intention in your good works is not sufficiently pure and detached from the regard of the world. Do good without expecting a return. Occupy yourself so completely with the good work itself that you do not ever think about what will come to you from it. Leave everything to God's judgment, so that he alone sees you, while you hide from yourself.

"Sound no trumpet before you" (Matt. 6:2), like those who endlessly talk about what they do and say. They are themselves their own trumpet, so greatly do they fear not being seen by men.

Week 2: Wednesday

Not to Be Served

The hour of Jesus approaches. He goes up to Jerusalem voluntarily, knowing that he will die there, and he says so to his Apostles.

"Then the mother of the sons of Zebedee came up to him, with her sons, and kneeling before him . . . she said to him, 'Command that these two sons of mine may sit, one at your right hand and one at your left, in your kingdom'" (Matt. 20:20-21). In recounting the same episode, St. Mark says plainly that it was not only their mother, but the two brothers themselves, that is, Sts. James and John, who made the request (Mark 10:35-37). This shows us that their mother was acting at the instigation of her sons, who seem to have joined openly in the demand. And this is why the Savior addressed his response to them: "Are you able to drink the cup that I am to drink?" (Matt. 20:22).

This exchange shows us how hard it was for the apostles to hear about the Cross. Jesus has just spoken of it clearly (Matt. 20:19), and far from hearing it, Sts. James and John — leaders among the Apostles — have just spoken to him of his glory and of the distinction that they hope to gain from him.

Let us weigh these words of Jesus: "You do not know what you are asking" (Matt. 20:22). You speak of glory, and you are not thinking about what must be suffered in order to gain it. Then he explains these sufferings to them by two metaphors, by that of the bitter cup that must be drunk and by the bloody baptism that must be accepted. To swallow every sort of bitterness, to be suffering to the point of having one's body submerged, as in baptism: this is the price of glory.

The ambitious apostles offer themselves for all of it, but Jesus, who can see that they are only offering to suffer from ambition, does not choose to satisfy them. He grants their request so far as the Cross is concerned, but as to glory, he refers them to the eternal decrees and hidden wisdom of his Father. He might have said to them what he subsequently said to all the Apostles: "As my Father appointed a kingdom for me, so do I appoint one for you" (cf. Luke 22:29). But those who are willing to suffer only for ambition were not yet worthy to hear this promise. So, to attach them to the Cross, the power of which they did not yet comprehend, Jesus leaves to the Father what pertains to glory and here allows himself only to predict and distribute afflictions.

All of this was accomplished with the profound economy so often practiced in the Gospel, where, for various reasons, different things are attributed to the Father and to the Son. Yet we must always remember that what lies beneath as foundation is what the Savior said to his Father: "All mine are Thine, and Thine are mine" (cf. John 17:10).

The other apostles "were indignant" at the two brothers' request (Matt. 20:24). Blind, they did not realize that they were all possessed by the same sentiments they condemned in the two, inasmuch as both earlier and later Jesus surprised them in a dispute as to "which of them was the greatest" (Luke 9:46; 22:24). So it is that we cannot endure in others the vice that we have in ourselves: we are sufficiently keen sighted to levy reproof, but too blind for self-knowledge and self-correction.

We should take note of the admirable change that the Savior's instructions and the effusion of the Holy Spirit effected in the Apostles. These men who never stopped arguing among themselves about who was the greatest, effortlessly ceded the honor to St. Peter. They let him speak everywhere. He presided at all their councils and assemblies. St. John, who had just asked for the first place, waits for St. Peter at the Savior's tomb so that he can go in first, and his haste to see the signs of the Resurrection of his Master did not prevent him from paying the honor that he owed to the prince of the Apostles.

Let us consider well the words of St. Matthew by which Jesus casts down all ambition by his example:

> You know that the rulers of the Gentiles lord it over them, and their great men exercise authority over them. It shall not be so among you; but whoever would be great among you must be your servant, and whoever would be first among you must be your slave, even as the Son of man came not to be served but to serve, and to give his life as a ransom for many. (Matt. 20:25-28)

Do not be ambitious, O Christian! Do not desire to command or to have any advantage among men, for you are the disciple of the One who, although Lord of all, made himself a servant and placed all of his glory in the redemption of his elect by the loss of his life. Redeemed by the humility and the Cross of your Savior, do not dream of elevating yourself, nor puffing up your heart in any way.

Let us also consider how much our passions blind us, especially ambition, and let us cry out, like the two blind men and like Bartimaeus: "Lord, let our eyes be opened" (Matt. 20:33; Mark 10:46, 51; Luke 18:41). Help us to know our faults. The reproach of men must never prevent us from crying out to Jesus to implore the help of his grace. Let us leave behind our habits, run to him, open our eyes, glorify God, and let us never glory in ourselves.

Jeremiah: A Type of Christ

Jeremiah's tears were a continual intercession for his people. "Let my eyes run down with tears night and day, and let them not cease, for the virgin daughter of my people is smitten with a great wound, with a very grievous blow. If I go out into the field, behold, those slain by the sword! And if I enter the city, behold, the diseases of famine! Hast thou utterly rejected Judah? Does thy soul loathe Zion? Why hast thou smitten us so that there is no healing for us? We looked for peace, but no good came; for a time of healing, but behold, terror. We acknowledge our wickedness, O Lord, and the iniquity of our fathers, for we have sinned against thee. Do not spurn us, for thy name's sake; do not dishonor thy glorious throne" (cf. Jer. 14:17-21). "Though our iniquities testify against us," and set themselves in opposition to the mercy we beg of you, nevertheless "act, O Lord, for thy name's sake" (cf. Jer. 14:7). "Remember and do not break thy covenant with us" (cf. Jer. 14:21). Alas, O Lord, will we find a God like you among the peoples who surround us in our exile? "Are there any among the false gods of the nations that can bring rain? Or can the heavens give showers? Art thou not he, O Lord our God? We set our hope on thee, for thou doest all these things" (cf. Jer. 14:22).

So did Jeremiah pray day and night, with tears and groaning, for a people that had not ceased to injure him and seek his death. He was a type of Christ, our great high priest, who "in the days of his flesh," of his weakness, suffering, and mortal life, "offered up prayers and supplications, with loud cries and tears" to his Father, and "was heard for his godly fear" (Heb. 5:7), until at last, upon the Cross to which his own people had affixed him, he cried out: "Father, forgive them; for they know not what they do" (Luke 23:34).

God enabled Jeremiah to do what Jesus Christ would one day command: "Pray for those who persecute you" (Matt. 5:44). "Is evil a recompense for good?" (Jer. 18:20), he asked. Why have they "dug a pit for my life"; have I not been tirelessly at work for their good? "Remember, O Lord, how I stood before thee to speak good for them, to turn away thy wrath from them" (Jer. 18:20). In truth, this speech of Jeremiah seems to have been followed by terrible imprecations against the people; but we know that according to the style of the prophets, even this, under the figure of imprecation, is only a manner of predicting the evils to befall these ingrates in the future. This is why we see the same prophet, when he sees the evils that he has predicted come to pass, is far from being joyful — as he would have been had he wished for them to suffer — but is instead brought to tears by the sight of their disaster, and finishes his lamentations with this prayer: "Remember, O Lord, what has befallen us; behold, and see our disgrace! Why dost thou forget us forever, why dost thou so long forsake us? Restore us to thyself, O Lord, that we may be restored! Renew our days as of old! Or hast thou utterly rejected us? Art thou exceedingly angry with us?" (cf. Lam. 5:1, 20-22).

Week 2: Friday

The Wicked Tenants

"Hear another parable" (Matt. 21:33). He speaks to us as well as to the Jews. Let us listen then, and let us see the entire history of the Church under the simplest figure imaginable.

"There was a householder who planted a vineyard" (Matt. 21:33). It was David who sang of it: "Thou didst bring a vine out of Egypt; thou didst drive out the nations and plant it.... It took deep root and filled the land. The mountains were covered with its shade, the mighty cedars with its branches; it sent out its branches to the sea, and its shoots to the river" (cf. Ps. 80:8-11). Here is something even clearer in Isaiah: "My beloved," that is, my anointed Son, the Christ, "had a vineyard on a very fertile hill," and he "planted it with choice vines; he built a watchtower in the midst of it," for those who would care for it, and he "hewed out a wine vat in it" (Isa. 5:1-2). These are the very words of our Savior.

"He let it out to tenants" (Matt. 21:33). He committed the tending of it to the priests, the sons of Aaron, and to the doctors of the Law.

"He sent his servants to the tenants to get his fruit" (Matt. 21:34). "I have sent to you all my servants the prophets" (Jer. 35:15), in morning and evening, to warn the princes, the priests, and the people, that they ought to give to God the fruit he expects from the tending he had given to his vineyard with the Law and the Sacred Scriptures. Instead of listening to the prophets, they persecuted and killed them (Matt. 23:34). "Which of the prophets did not your fathers persecute?" St. Stephen asked them. "They killed those who announced beforehand the coming of the Righteous One, whom you have now betrayed and murdered" (Acts 7:52). This is just what Jesus reproaches them for in this parable.

After all the prophets, "he sent his son," Christ himself, saying, "They will respect my son" (Matt. 21:37). He had what he needed to make himself respected: his admirable doctrine and his miracles. Nevertheless, they dragged him from the vineyard, from Jerusalem, onto Calvary, and they had him brutally slain by the Romans.

We should marvel at the way that Jesus boldly challenges them with this parable, revealing their schemes, what they will accomplish in just two days. Should they not have been moved by his discourse? And all the more since the Savior placed their very crime so plainly before their eyes, so that when he asked them what the house-holder would do in that case, they were constrained to respond: "He will put those wretches to a miserable death, and let out the vineyard to other tenants" (Matt. 21:41). Which he then proceeded to explain, saying, "The king-dom of God will be taken away from you and given to a nation producing the fruits of it" (Matt. 21:43). This is indeed what soon happened, as the Apostles told them: "It was necessary that the word of God should be spoken first to you. Since you thrust it from you, and judge your-selves unworthy of eternal life, behold, we turn to the Gentiles. For so the Lord has commanded us, saying, 'I have set you to be a light for the Gentiles'" (Acts 13:46-7; cf. Isaiah 49:6).

Let us not mistake our Savior's purposes: since we are the nation he has chosen to bear the fruit of his word, let us be fruitful in good works. "The fruit of the Spirit is love, joy, peace, patience, kindness, goodness, faith-fulness, gentleness, self-control" (Gal. 5:22). These are the fruits we must bear, and not the works of the flesh that bear the fruit of death, which are "immorality, impu-rity, enmity, strife, drunkenness, carousing" and the oth-ers that St. Paul lists in the same place (Gal. 5:19-21).

Otherwise the kingdom of God will be taken from us as it was taken from the Jews, and another will "seize our crown" (cf. Rev. 3:11). "For if God did not spare" the Jews, who were "the natural branches, neither will he spare you" (Rom. 11:21). This was the great sadness of the Jews: to see the crown that had been destined to them placed in the hands of the Gentiles, when, as the Savior said, "many will come from east and west and sit at table with Abraham, Isaac, and Jacob in the kingdom of heaven, while the sons of the kingdom will be thrown into the outer darkness; there men will weep and gnash their teeth" (Matt. 8:11-12). For they will see the place that they should have had, the crown that they should have worn, and they will see their place filled by others and their crown on other heads. Then they will cry futile tears, and they will be enraged to the point of grinding their teeth. Listen, Christian! Read your destiny in that of the Jews, but read it and listen in your heart, and do not allow so clear a parable to be unheeded.

O my God! You have destined this crown for me. Let me quickly wrest it from your hands: it will not perish, for you know to whom you have given it, you know your elect, and the number of them will be complete. Place me among the number of those who will not lose their crown.

The Love of God for Repentant Sinners

Consider the old saying: "If a man divorces his wife and she goes from him and becomes another man's wife, will he return to her? Would not that land be greatly polluted?" And you, sinning soul, "you have played the harlot with many lovers" (Jer. 3:1). It is not I who have left you, says the Lord. No, I am a faithful spouse, one who never sues for divorce. But you, faithless soul, you have abandoned me and given yourself not to a single lover, but to thousands upon thousands of corruptors. Nevertheless, if you come back to me, says the Lord, I will receive you.

"Lift up your eyes," and, as far as your sight can reach, you will see the marks of your infamy. Shall I repeat for you the list of your desires for vengeance, your envies, your secret hatreds, the ambition to which you have sacrificed everything, your impure and disordered loves? "You have polluted the land with your vile harlotry. You have a harlot's brow, you refuse to be ashamed" (Jer. 3:2-3).

Come back to me; henceforth call me your father, your spouse, and the protector of your purity. Why do you wish to be far from me, like an errant bride? Will you persist in your unjust anger? You said that you would do evil, you boasted of it, and you have done it, you have been capable of it. I abandoned you to your ways. "Return," faithless one. "I will not look upon you in anger, for I am merciful. I will not be angry forever. Only acknowledge your guilt, that you rebelled against the Lord your God and scattered your favors among strangers under every green tree," that there was no vain pleasure that did not mislead you, "and that you have not obeyed my voice, says the Lord. Return, O faithless children" (Jer. 3:12-14). Return.

Return to the paternal home, prodigal child. You shall be given the best garments. A feast shall be given for your return. The whole house shall rejoice, and your father, moved by his deep tenderness, will explain himself to the just ones who never left him, saying: "You are always with me," but "it was fitting to make merry and be glad, for this your brother was dead, and is alive; he was lost, and is found" (Luke 15:31-12). Rejoice with me, and with the heavens above, where there are celebrations for the conversion of sinners, and understand that "there will be more joy in heaven over one sinner who repents than over ninety-nine righteous persons who need no repentance" (Luke 15:7).

"Come back, O faithless children," come back, unfaithful spouses, "for I am your master" (Jer. 3:14). Is it my will that the impious perish or rather that he return to me and live? Return to me, repent, and your sin will not lead you to ruin. Depart from all of your lies and disobedience and make yourselves a new heart and a new spirit. Why should you wish to die, O house of Israel? "Have I any pleasure in the death of the wicked?" No, says the Lord, "I have no pleasure in the death of any one; so turn, and live" (Ezek. 18:23, 32).

"I, I am he who blots out your transgressions for my own sake," and to satisfy my own goodness: "and I will not remember your sins," only you must "put me in remembrance." "Let us argue together," for I am willing to lower myself to you. "Set forth your case"; shall you "be proved right" after I have pardoned you so many times? (Isa. 43:25-56). "Remember these things, O Jacob," and do not forget me. "I have swept away your transgressions like a cloud," and chased away your sins as the sun burns off the fog. Sinners, "return to me, for I have redeemed you. Sing, O heavens. Shout, O depths of the earth; break forth into singing, O mountains, O forest, and every tree in it!" For the Lord has had mercy upon us (Isa. 44:21-23).

"For as the heavens are high above the earth," so high has he lifted up his mercy; "as far as the east is from the west, so far does he remove our transgressions from us. As a father pities his children," so God has had pity on us, because he knows our weaknesses and that we are made of the stuff of the earth. We are nothing but mud and dust; our days "are like grass" (Ps. 103:11-15). We wilt like the flowers, and our souls, still more fragile than our bodies, are entirely lacking in strength.

Week 3: Sunday

In Spirit and in Truth

My Savior, because considering the vain speech of those who reject your Church leads me to desire a greater understanding of your truth, I wish to reflect upon the arguments that are made against the adoration, reservation, and exposition of your Blessed Sacrament.

They say that the words of the Gospel do not show that the Apostles adored the Body and Blood of Jesus Christ when they received them. Let us ask them whether we see the Apostles adoring Jesus himself, who was constantly seated with them in his visible and natural form.

O my God! Will not these disputatious souls see that whichever way they respond they will convict themselves? Did the Apostles adore Jesus? If they say yes, then they believe it without its being written down. If they say no, then what shall they conclude about the fact that it is not written down whether they adored the Eucharist?

These misbelievers, thinking themselves to be wise and calling us fools, are themselves the fools, for they know nothing about true adoration. Let us restrict ourselves to the very words that are written about the Last Supper, and without supplementing the account with reference to other passages in the Gospels, let us believe Jesus when he says: "Take, eat; this is my body" (Matt. 26:26). Believe him, that is, without hesitating and without arguing, when he says something so astonishing. Do what he says and eat what appears to be bread with a sure faith that it is his true body. Do the same with the sacred chalice.

To make an act of faith, at once so pure and so exalted: is this not to adore Jesus Christ? But to discern with St. Paul that this is not only the body of a man, but that of God, and the true bread come down from Heaven, to place our hope and to seek our life there, to bind ourselves to him by love: is this not perfect adoration? What does it mean to add to such a faith genuflections, bows, prostrations, or any manner of exterior adoration except to pay outward witness to what is in our heart?

"Do you believe in the Son of man?" said the Savior to the blind man he had healed. "Who is he," he replied, "that I may believe in him?" "It is he who speaks to you," responded Jesus. And the man born blind said, "'Lord, I believe'; and he worshiped him" (John 9:35-38). What did he do by prostrating himself before Jesus except to repeat in another manner and another language the "I believe" he had just spoken with his mouth? That woman who touched him in order to be healed (Luke 8:43): had she not already adored him in her heart before throwing herself at his feet?

Who does not see that to believe in Jesus, who says, "This is my body; this is my blood," to receive him in this faith, and to discern that this body is God's body by which life is given to us is already an act of the highest adoration and that all the prostrations that we make to Jesus Christ are only its outward witness? It is then with good reason that we join the exterior to the interior adoration of the Eucharist, that is, that we join sign to sentiment and testimony to faith. It is with good reason, as the saints tell us, that we make manifest without, by our posture, the humility of our spirit within, and that, as St. Augustine says, "no one takes this body without having first adored it." The Church's witness to this practice is constant. But why do we seek these witnesses when to eat and to drink this Body and Blood, as the Body and Blood of God, and to place all our hope in it is already so exalted a form of adoration that we see it must pull all the others behind it in its train?

Let us take the step. Let us tarry no longer. Let us adore Jesus, who reposes upon the altar. Ah! It is there that he awaits me. It is from thence that he shall one day be brought to me as Viaticum, to bring me happily from this life to the next. Bread of those who seek, you will one day be the bread of those who see, the bread of those who live in the heavenly fatherland. I adore you. I believe in you. I desire you. I commune with you in spirit: you are my nourishment; you are my life.

Week 3: Monday

The Silence of Christ

Let us consider that the silence of patience in affliction, suffering, and contradiction is one of the most difficult parts of Christian morality to practice.

Few people like to suffer, and to suffer in silence in the sight of God alone. And if it is rare to find those who like to suffer, it is still rarer to find those who suffer without trying to tell the world of it. It is silence, however, that sanctifies our crosses and our afflictions and greatly increases their merit. If you find it difficult to suffer your crosses and defeats, bring Jesus to mind. Amid an infinite number of persecutions and sorrows that he endured in the presence of his wicked judges, before whom he was so falsely accused and slandered, he responded not at all: "Jesus was silent" (Matt. 26:63). His profound silence and invincible patience astonished Pontius Pilate: "the governor wondered greatly" (Matt. 27:14). Jesus endured a thousand injuries, insults, and indignities from all manner of persons. He was falsely accused by his cruel enemies, the scribes and the Pharisees. They said he was a blasphemer, a rebel, a breaker of the law, and a disturber of the peace, that he had contempt for the Roman taxes, and, finally, that he was misleading the people with his new doctrine. His sacred ears rang with these outcries and calumnies, but Jesus did not say a single word to justify or defend himself against these angry dogs who were so outrageously shredding his reputation. And in that dark night when this dear Savior suffered an infinite number of injuries, affronts, and cruelties: what did this mild lamb say? Alas! Not the least impatient word.

Then, in that bloody and sorrowful scourging, when he was slashed and striped by the lash, which made blood stream from his sacred veins: what patience and silence did this mild Jesus show then! He suffered all this without saying a word. He did not so much as open his mouth to complain of the cruelty of his proud executioners, who were still not content with the inhumanity they had dealt out to him.

So they took a sharp crown of thorns and pierced him to the skull. Jesus endured this torment like the others, with an unbreakable silence. He was led to Herod, who greatly desired to see him and who rejoiced. But our Lord constantly persevered in keeping a profound silence.

The Silence of Christ

Although he knew full well that Herod had the power to hand him over to his enemies, he said not a word in his presence: a marvel. It was with good reason that one of the Fathers called him the victim of silence; Jesus consecrated silence by the patience he displayed in his Passion.

We should admire and imitate his example. This is how we should behave when we are wrongly accused and persecuted. In whatever condition God allows you to be, and amid whatever pain he allows, learn how to remain with him without seeking consolation from creatures. Take the part of silence and shut yourself up within so that our Lord can give you the interior strength to suffer virtuously and meritoriously. It is upon these occasions that we must say with David: "My soul refused to be comforted: I remembered God, and was delighted" (Ps. 76:3-4, Douay-Rheims [RSV = Ps. 77:3-4]).

It is here that our souls are tested and marvelously improved when, by a truly Christian generosity, we are able to rise up above all that troubles and opposes us, and, like Jesus, we keep a profound silence, even when there is something to speak about, whether for our justification against an unjust accusation, or amid a raging tempest of trouble. A truly generous soul must defend itself with silence, which will be its calm and peace amid the storm. Jesus will send an interior sweetness into the depths of the hearts of those who, by a little courage, reject and abandon the help of creatures for the sake of his love.

In our sufferings and contradictions, let us not look to secondary causes. We must not pander to our self-love by a vain search for someone to blame for our sufferings. We must instead lift our sights to Heaven, to see that it is God himself who has allowed these things to happen to us, and that they will be for the sake of our salvation if we know how to profit from them. In all of the most vexing occurrences, a truly Christian soul should say to God from the depths within: "My heart is ready, O God, my heart is ready" (Ps. 107:2, Douay-Rheims [RSV = Ps. 108:1]). I am ready to do your will, come what may.

Week 3: Tuesday

Reconciliation

We can learn how much God loves peace from the beautiful precept that commands us to be reconciled with our brother before we worship, lest we approach the oblation offered to him with a resentful heart and hands bent upon vengeance.

We should be most attentive to these words: "If you are offering your gift at the altar, and there remember that your brother has something against you, leave your gift there before the altar and go; first be reconciled to your brother, and then come and offer your gift" (Matt. 5:23-24). And we should seek reconciliation not only when we have actually offended our brother, but even if he has taken offense mistakenly. We should seek a charitable resolution for fear that we might come to hate him, should we discover that he already hates us. The first gift to offer to God is a heart that is cleansed of all coldness and of all unfriendliness toward our brother.

We should not wait for Sunday, whether we are all together or by ourselves alone at Holy Mass. The Lord's Day should be preceded by reconciliation.

We must carry to still greater lengths our love of peace. St. Paul says, "Do not let the sun go down on your anger" (Eph. 4:26). The shadows only cause our annoyance to increase. Our anger will return and awaken us in the night, and it will have become embittered. The somber, sorrowful emotions—among which are hatred, the desire for vengeance, and jealousy—become more painful during the night in the same way that wounds and fevers and illnesses do.

In quarrels, lawsuits, and disputes, each summons the other before a judge, because the offense is mutual. Both parties ought instead to seek a voluntary and mutual settlement, rather than to arrive at a judgment that will only increase the bitterness of all. This is the truth that we must consider.

St. Augustine said that the enemy with whom we must be reconciled while we are wayfarers here below is none other than the truth, which condemns us in this life, and in the next brings us to the executioner who will oblige us to pay to the last penny, that is to say, to remain forever in that appalling prison, for we will never be able to satisfy the debt of our crimes.

Reconciliation

"Forgive us our debts, as we also have forgiven our debtors" (Matt. 6:12, Douay-Rheims). It is something worthy of our reflection that God has made the pardon that we hope for from him depend upon the pardon that he commands us to give to those who have offended us. Not content to have constantly inculcated this obligation, he has placed it in our own mouths in our daily prayer, so that should we fail to pardon, he will say to us what he said to the wicked servant: "I condemn you out of your own mouth!" (cf. Luke 19:22). You asked pardon from me, promising to pardon in return. You have pronounced your own sentence when you refused to pardon your brother. Get thee to that unhappy place where there is neither pardon nor mercy.

Not One Iota

Christian life demands extreme precision. We must carefully observe even the smallest precepts and disdain none of them. When we slacken in little things, we fall into greater evils. "He who despises small things will fail little by little" (Sir. 19:1).

To establish the high ideal of Christian justice, Jesus lays down this admirable principle: "Till heaven and earth pass away, not an iota, not a dot, will pass from the law until all is accomplished" (Matt. 5:18).

He has in view here what was foretold about him in the Law and the prophets, which is why he says, "I have come … to fulfill them" (Matt. 5:17). As to what was foretold in the law, here are the chief points: the birth of Christ from a virgin, his suffering, his Cross, his Resurrection, the conversion of the world and of the Gentiles and the reprobation and just punishment of the Jews. These are the chief points, but not all, for there is the iota as well, that is, each minor point. These also must be accomplished. It was necessary that his garments be divided and that the soldiers gamble for his tunic.

See the great precision in so subtle a point: this is the iota, the smallest letter. He will be sold — that is perhaps a great point — but that it should be for thirty pieces of silver, that the potter's field should be bought with it: these are the iota, the smallest letter, and it should not be overlooked. It was the same with the requirement that he thirst and that he be slaked with vinegar. He would suffer: that is a chief point. But that it should take place outside the city: that is the iota. He will be sacrificed like the Paschal lamb, but his bones will no more be broken on the Cross than those of the lamb were: again, the iota.

Jesus means that everything said by way of foreshadowing in the Law will be accomplished in truth in the Gospel, even to the least circumstances. Everything in the Law, even the smallest detail, is significant, and everything, even the smallest detail, will be accomplished in the Gospel. "You shall not muzzle an ox when it treads out the grain" (Deut. 25:4). St. Paul applies this to preachers (1 Tim. 5:18). It is the same with other matters. "You shall not boil a kid in its mother's milk" (Deut. 14:21). "If you chance to come upon a bird's nest ... you shall not take the mother with the young; you shall let the mother go, but the young you may take." And "you shall not wear a mingled stuff, wool and linen together. You shall make yourself tassels on the four corners of your cloak" (Deut. 22:6-7, 11-12). Each of these little matters bears great significance as an encouragement to Christians to practice mildness, moderation, simplicity, uprightness, and every other virtue.

The conclusion that Jesus draws is that we must not forget even the least precepts. If everything that God foretold about his Son was accomplished down to the smallest letter, then we must always fulfill everything that has been foretold for us.

Consider to what extent this is true: "Heaven and earth will pass away, but my words will not pass away" (Matt. 24:35). If the sun were to disappear all at once, and the world's lamp were to be extinguished in the middle of the day, if the earth were to give way before our feet, and the once-solid foundation were to be reduced to powder, what misery would be ours! Everything would be lost. But how much greater is the evil if the least of the commandments of Jesus Christ be ignored.

Suffering restores order. Punishment for sin is the rule. You come to order through suffering, just as you stray by sinning. Sin without punishment would be the worst disorder, as the disorder not of the man who sins but of the

God who does not punish. This disorder will never come to pass, however, because God, who is the rule itself, cannot be unlawful.

As this rule is perfect, perfectly straight and without the least bend, anything that does not conform to it breaks upon it and will feel its invincible and immutable rectitude.

But if the threats are to be accomplished, the promises will be as well. Go to your crucifix: look upon it and see all of the predictions accomplished, even the least of them. Say to yourself: everything will be fulfilled, and the happiness that has been promised to me will not fail. I will see God, I will love him, I will praise him forever and ever, and all my desires will be fulfilled, all my hopes accomplished. Amen. Amen.

Priest, Prophet, and King

Although what we owe to Jesus is included in the commandment to love God, it is nevertheless worth considering what we owe to him as the Christ, that is, as the mediator and bond of God's love for us and ours for him. To do this we should look to Christ's own explanation of the famous prophecy of his reign spoken by David his forefather.

How lovely it is that the Christ should have been seen by his fathers! By Abraham, who saw his day and rejoiced in it (John 8:56), and by David, who was stunned by his grandeur and called "my Lord" (Ps. 110:1) one who would be his own son.

As God gave to Abraham the promise of the multiplication of the faithful, so he gave to David that of his eternal kingdom, of a throne that would outlast the sun and the moon (Ps. 89:35-7). Thus it was fitting that David—to whom as a figure of Jesus Christ the promise was made — would be the first to recognize the Christ by calling him his Lord. "The Lord said to my Lord" (Ps. 110:1); it is as if he had said, "It appears that God has promised a never-ending empire to me, but, in truth, it is to you, my son and also my Lord, to whom it shall be given. And I come in spirit, the first of all your subjects, to pay you homage upon your throne, at the right hand of your Father, as to my sovereign Lord."

"If David thus calls him Lord, how is he his son?" (Matt. 22:45). By this question, Jesus wished to lift their sights to the higher birth of the Christ, who was not merely the Son of David, but the only-begotten Son of God. All they had to do in order to learn of this eternal birth was to continue the psalm, for God himself says in what follows: "In the brightness of the saints; from the womb before the dawn I begot thee" (Ps. 109:3, Douay-Rheims [RSV = Ps. 110:3]).

Before the dawn, before that light that sets and rises every day had begun to appear, there was an eternal light that made the happiness of the saints: it is in this eternal light that I have begotten you.

I adore you, O Jesus, my Lord, in this immense and eternal light. I adore you as the light that "enlightens every man" (John 1:9): God from God, light from light, true God from true God.

What a joy it is to see Jesus Christ himself explaining the prophecies that touch upon him and thus teaching us how we should understand all the others. All that we owe to Jesus is shown to us in this psalm. We see him first as God, and we say: this is our God, and there is no other. For if he has been begotten, he is the Son; if he is the Son, he is of the same nature as the Father; if he is the same nature as his Father, he is God, and one God alone with his Father, for nothing is more essential to God than his unity.

He is king. Where is his throne? At the right hand of God. Could it be placed any higher? Everything depends upon this throne, all that depends upon God and the kingdom of Heaven is submitted to him: here is his reign.

This empire is a sacred one, a priesthood, and a priesthood established by an oath. God willed by a more particular declaration of his will to mark this priesthood as unique: "The Lord has sworn and will not change his mind." The priesthood of Jesus Christ is eternal: "You are a priest for ever according to the order of Melchizedek" (Ps. 110:4). You have neither beginning nor end. This is not a priesthood that came from your ancestors, nor one that will pass to your descendants. Your priesthood will not pass to other hands: there will be priests who will sacrifice under you, but they will be your vicars and not your successors.

You celebrate an eternal office for us at the right hand of your Father. You continually hold up the marks of the wounds that appeased him and save us. You offer him our prayers. You intercede for our faults. You bless and consecrate us. From the heights of Heaven you baptize your children. You change earthly gifts into your Body and Blood. You take away our sins. You send your Holy Spirit, consecrate your ministers, and accomplish all that they perform in your name. When we are born, you wash us with heavenly water; when we die, you support us with the comfort of your anointing, and our sufferings become our remedies, our death a passage to true life. O God! O King! O High Priest! I unite myself to you in all of these qualities and submit myself to your divinity, your rule, and your priesthood, which I honor in humility and faith in the person of those by whom you are pleased to exercise it on earth.

Week 3: Friday

The Great Commandment

"Teacher, which is the great commandment in the law?" (Matt. 22:36). Jesus, who is the truth itself, always proceeded directly to the first principle. It was clear that the greatest commandment should have to do with God, which is why he chose this passage for his answer: "Hear, O Israel: the Lord our God is one Lord" (Deut. 6:4). Here God's greatness is proclaimed in his perfect unity, from which it follows that we ought to consecrate to him our love, thus making him reign in our hearts. The love that we must give to so perfect a being should also be perfect. This is why the Savior answered the question by referring to the Scripture passage that commands the perfect union of all of our desires in God. Yet for fear that an ignorant person might suspect that binding all of our love together into our love for God would leave none for our neighbor, he added the second precept to the first, carrying the love of neighbor to its perfection by again showing that the

The Great Commandment

law commands that we "love our neighbor as ourselves" and using the word *neighbor* instead of the word *friend* that is in the law (cf. Lev. 19:18 in the Douay-Rheims), because the more general word *neighbor* extends our charity to all those who share our common nature, as the Son of God had already explained in the parable of the Good Samaritan (Luke 10:29).

Here, then, we see the entire law summed up in its two most general principles. Man is thus perfectly instructed about all his duties, for he sees in the blink of an eye what he owes to God, his Creator, and to men, his equals. Here is the whole Decalogue: the first table is contained in the precept to love God, and the second in the love of neighbor. Not only is the Decalogue contained in these two precepts, but "all the law and the prophets" (Matt. 22:40), for God here teaches us not only our exterior duties, but also the inner principle by which we ought to act, which is love. The one who loves lacks in nothing toward the one whom he loves. And he instructs us gently, not obliging us to read and to understand the entire law—which the weak and the ignorant would not be able to do—but instead reducing the whole to six lines. Moreover, lest our attention be dissipated by considering each of our duties in particular, he includes them all in the single principle of a sincere love, by saying that we must "love the Lord your God with all your heart ... and your neighbor as yourself" (Matt. 22:37-39).

Let us adore eternal truth in this admirable abridgement of the law. How indebted to you am I, O Lord, who gives me the whole substance of the law in just a few words! When, to give my mind its suitable exercise, I read the rest of your Scriptures, these two precepts will be the thread that leads me through all of the difficulties of that profound book. They will resolve and untangle every difficulty. O God, I praise you! O Jesus, be blessed! O Jesus, I will apply myself to meditating upon this admirable summary of heavenly doctrine. I wish to meditate on these words so full of light, so that I may be sensible of their power and fill myself with them. O Jesus, give me that grace! O Jesus, fill my soul with your Holy Spirit, which is the eternal and subsistent love of your Father and of yourself, so that he may teach me to love you both, and to love with you, as one and the same God, the Spirit that proceeds from you both.

Through Christ Our Lord

"If you abide in me, and my words abide in you, ask whatever you will, and it shall be done for you" (John 15:7). Whoever would pray ought to take to heart these words: "Apart from me you can do nothing" (John 15:5). Nothing. Nothing at all. We pray, we beg, because we have nothing and consequently can do nothing, or, to say it all in a single word, because we *are* nothing. So we must pray, knowing that we are heard only in the name of Jesus, but also that in his name we can obtain all.

Here are two truths about prayer. The first is that we are not heard for ourselves, but in the name of Jesus Christ. The second is that we neither can nor ought to pray by our own spirit, but by the Spirit of Jesus Christ. Not only should we pray in the way that Jesus taught us and by asking only for what he wants us to ask, but even more should we recognize that it is he himself who forms our prayer in us by his Spirit. Without him we cannot pray at all, as St. Paul explained: "The Spirit helps us in our weakness; for we do not know how to pray as we ought, but the Spirit himself intercedes for us with sighs too deep for words" (Rom. 8:26).

Even as we keep before us this first truth—"apart from me you can do nothing"—we should also attend to this other one: "I can do all things in him who strengthens me" (Phil. 4:13). I can do nothing apart from Jesus Christ, and I can do everything with Jesus Christ and in his name. This is why we always hear the prayers of the Church conclude with these words that are as humble as they are consoling: "through Christ our Lord." Confessing our powerlessness, these words humble us; revealing the source of our strength, they console. They are the necessary conclusion even when we pray for the intercession of our Lady and the saints, who have no merit, no dignity, no glory except through Jesus Christ and his name.

We must take care lest we imagine that it suffices merely to repeat the words "through Christ our Lord." We must say them from the depths of our hearts, by remaining in Christ and by Christ's remaining in us. That is to say, by attaching ourselves to him with our whole hearts, with a lively and firm faith, and by his remaining in us by his word being impressed in our heart, and by his

Spirit impelling and animating our prayer. For he does not dwell in us without acting, as St. Paul said: "He is not weak in dealing with you, but is powerful in you" (2 Cor. 13:3).

This, then, is how we truly pray in the name of Christ: when we remain in him and he in us, allowing ourselves to be led to him, to be silent, to listen to what he says in us, so that we may practice truly and intimately what he says: "If you remain in me, and my word"—not only the word spoken externally, but the one that I hear in the depths of my heart—"remains in you." Then we will obtain what we desire.

Now, this word that is to remain in us should chiefly be the word of the Cross, which is the one that this discourse has in view. For Jesus was going to the Cross, and leading his disciples there with him, as what follows in the Gospel reveals. We must understand that to remain in Christ is to remain in the word of his Cross, and for the word of his Cross to remain in us, and that to pray in the name of Jesus Christ is to make supplication through his blood and his sufferings, by loving them and taking part in them.

Week 4: Sunday

A Life Hidden in God (I)

"You have died, and your life is hidden with Christ in God. When Christ who is our life appears, then you also will appear with him in glory" (Col. 3:3-4).

You have died: to what? To sin. You have died to it by baptism, by repentance, and by the profession of a Christian life. You have died to sin, but how then can "we who died to sin still live in it?" (Rom. 6:2). We must die to it once and for all.

In order to die to sin completely, it is necessary that we die to all of our bad inclinations, to all that flatters our senses, and to pride. For all these things the Scriptures call sin, because they come from sin, because they incline to sin, and because they do not allow us to be entirely free from sin.

"You have died." When shall these words of St. Paul be accomplished in us? At what blessed moment of our lives? When shall we be without sin? Never in the course of this life. To whom, then, is St. Paul speaking when he says, "You have died"? Is it to the souls of the just? Are they dead? Are they not, on the contrary, in the land of the living? It cannot be to them that St. Paul speaks; it is to us. The concupiscence of evil remains in us, and we must fight against it our entire lives. But we hold it fast, pinned to the ground. We hold it, but have we vanquished it? We ought to. We can, with the grace of God. And if during the struggle it deals some injury to us, we shall not cease groaning, nor humbling ourselves, saying with St. Paul, "Who will deliver me from this body of death?" (Rom. 7:24). You have been delivered, Christian soul: you have been delivered in hope.

"And your life is hidden." Our death, then, is not total. St. Paul explains: "If Christ is in you, although your bodies are dead because of sin," that is, the sin that once reigned in them and which has left behind its traces, "your spirits are alive because of righteousness," the righteousness that charity pours out into our hearts (Rom. 8:10). It is with respect to the life of Christian righteousness that St. Paul says, "and your life is hidden." Set free from human judgment, we should count as true only what God sees in us, what he knows, and what he judges. God does not judge as man does. Man sees only the countenance, only the exterior. God penetrates to the depths of our hearts. God does not change as man does. His judgment is in no way inconstant. He is the only one upon whom we should rely. How happy we are then, and how peaceful! We are no longer dazzled by appearances, or stirred up by opinions; we are united to the truth and depend upon it alone.

I am praised, blamed, treated with indifference, disdained, ignored, or forgotten; none of this can touch me. I will be no less than I am. Men and women want to play at being a creator. They want to give me existence in their opinion, but this existence that they want to give me is nothingness. It is an illusion, a shadow, an appearance, that is, at bottom, nothingness. What is this shadow, always following me, behind me, at my side? Is it me, or something that belongs to me? No. Yet does not this shadow seem to move with me? No matter: it is not me. So it is with the judgments of men: they would follow me everywhere, paint me, sketch me, make me move according to their whim, and, in the end, give me some sort of existence. But in the end, I know it well: this is only a flickering light that takes me from one side or the other, that lengthens, shortens, swells, or shrinks the shadow that follows me, that makes it appear in various ways and disappear without my gaining or losing anything of my own. And what is this image of myself that I see reflected in the flowing stream? It blurs and erases itself; it disappears when the water is stirred up, but what have I lost? Nothing but a useless amusement. So it is with the opinions and judgments men form according to their lights. Alas, not only do I amuse myself with them as with a game; I stop, and I take them for something serious and true, and this shadow, this fragile image troubles me and makes me anxious, and I believe myself to be losing something. But I am disabused of this error. I am content with a hidden life. How peaceful it is! Whether I truly live this Christian life of which St. Paul speaks, I do not know, nor can I know with certainty. But I hope that I do, and I trust in God's goodness to help me.

A Life Hidden in God (II)

My life is "hidden with Christ in God" (Col. 3:4). It is here that we must open our hearts in silence and peace in the consideration of the hidden life of Jesus.

The God of glory hides himself under the veil of a mortal nature: "all the treasures of wisdom and knowledge" are in him, but they "are hidden" (Col. 2:3). This is the first step. And the second is that he hides in the womb of a virgin, and the wonder of his virginal conception remains hidden under the veil of marriage. He caused John the Baptist to recognize him within his mother's womb, where he lay. "When the voice of your greeting came to my ears," said Elizabeth, "the child in my womb leaped for joy" (Luke 1:44). Will he at least show himself upon coming into the world? Yes, to the shepherds, but otherwise, it was never more true than at the time of his birth that "he was in the world, and the world was made through him, yet the world knew him not" (John 1:10). The whole universe ignored him; his childhood had nothing special about it. "How is it that this man has learning, when he has never studied?" (John 7:15). He appears only once, at the age of twelve, but still it is not said that he taught: "sitting among the teachers, listening to them and asking them questions." In truth, he did so learnedly, but it does not appear to be the case that he decided matters then, even though this was one of the reasons that he came among us. "All who heard him were amazed at his understanding and his answers," but he had begun by listening and asking (Luke 2:46-47).

After having shone for a moment like the sun breaking through dark clouds, he again plunged into voluntary obscurity. When he responded to his parents, who had been searching for him, "Did you not know that I must be in my Father's house?" they "did not understand" (Luke 2:49-50). Mary, to whom the angel announced his divine birth and his grand and eternal reign, was as if ignorant, inasmuch as she spoke not a word of them. All she did was to listen to what was said about her son and be astonished, just as St. Luke says: "His father and his mother marveled at what was said about him" (Luke 2:33). This was the time to hide the treasure that had been entrusted to them, and so we know very little about him from these thirty years: he was the son of a carpenter and a carpenter himself; he worked in the shop of the man who was thought to be his father; and he was obedient to his parents and served them in their home and at work just as the children of the other artisans. His condition, then, was that he was hidden in God, or rather, that God was hidden in him. We will participate in the perfection and the happiness of the hidden Christ if our life is hidden in God with him.

He came out of this holy and divine obscurity, and he appeared as the light of the world. But at the same time, the world—the enemy of the light that revealed its evil works—heaped calumny upon him from every side, like black vapors to overshadow him. There is no sort of falsehood that was not tried against Jesus. No one knew what to believe of him. He was called a prophet and a deceiver. Some said he was the Christ; others denied it. He was a man who loved pleasure, good meals, and good wine. He was a Samaritan, a heretic, impious, an enemy of the Temple and of the holy people. He delivered those possessed by the power of Beelzebub; he was himself possessed; he had an evil spirit. Can anything good come out of Galilee? We do not know where he comes from, but certainly not from God, for he does not observe the Sabbath; instead he cures men and works miracles on that day. Who is this man who comes into Jerusalem and the Temple with such fanfare? We do not know him: "so there was a division among the people over him" (John 7:43). Who knew you, O Jesus? "Truly, thou art a God who hidest thyself, O God of Israel, the Savior" (cf. Isa. 45:15).

Yet when the hour came to save the world, he could be hidden no longer: "He was despised and rejected by men; a man of sorrows, and acquainted with grief; and as one from whom men hide their faces" (Isa. 53:3). No one recognized him. He seemed even to forget himself: "My God, my God"—he no longer called him Father—"why hast thou forsaken me?" (cf. Matt. 27:46). What! Is this no longer the well-beloved Son who had said: "He who sent me is with me; he has not left me alone" (John 8:29)? And now he says, "Why hast thou forsaken me?" Covered with our sins and, as it were, become a sinner in our place, he seems to have forgotten himself, and this is why the psalmist adds in his name: "Far from my salvation are the words of my sins" (Ps. 21:2, Douay-Rheims [RSV = Ps. 22:2]).

He died. He descended into the tomb. Soon he departed, and Mary Magdalene could not find him: she had lost the body of her Master. After his Resurrection, he appeared and disappeared eight or ten times. He showed himself for the last time, and a cloud took him from our sight: we will never see him again. His glory is proclaimed throughout the world, but if he is the power of God for believers, he is a scandal to the Jews and folly to the Gentiles (cf. 1 Cor. 1:23). The world does not know him, does not wish to know him. All the earth is covered with his enemies and those who blaspheme him. Heresies grow up in the very bosom of his Church to disfigure his mysteries and doctrine. Error prevails in the world, and even among his disciples there are some who do not know him, for no one knows him, he told us, except those who keep his commandments. And who keeps them? The impious have multiplied beyond all number; they can no longer be counted. But your true disciples, O my Savior, how rare are they, how scattered throughout the earth, and even in your Church! Scandal mounts, and charity cools. We seem to be living in the times you predicted: "When the Son of man comes, will he find faith on earth?" (Luke 18:8). But you do not thunder; you do not make us feel your might. Mankind blasphemes with impunity. Were we to judge according to human standards, we would think nothing more equivocal or dubious than your glory. It is found only in God, where you are hidden. And I, too, wish to be hidden in God with you.

Week 4: Tuesday

A Life Hidden in God (III)

My Lord, where shall you take me? What new light shall you shine upon me? I see the accomplishment of what the holy Simeon said: "Behold, this child is set for the fall and for the resurrection of many in Israel, and for a sign which shall be contradicted" (Luke 2:34, Douay-Rheims). O my Savior, what do I see in these words? The character of the Christ who was to come, his grandeur and divinity.

It is a form of God's grandeur that he should be knowable in so many ways and yet so little known, to shine forth in his works and yet be ignored by his creatures. From his goodness he spoke to mankind and did not leave them without revelation; but from his justice and grandeur he hides himself from the proud, who do not deign to open their eyes to see him. What need has he for their recognition? He needs only himself. Our knowing him is not a gift we give to him, but a grace he gives to us. We are amply punished if we refuse to see him. His essential glory is entirely in himself, and the glory he receives from men is a good for them, not for him.

Conversely, it is an evil for them, and the greatest of all evils, not to glorify him. Even a refusal to glorify him glorifies him in another way, because men make themselves unhappy by not knowing him. What does it matter to the sun whether we see it? Woe to the blind to whom its light is hidden; woe to the weak who cannot stand it! The blind man will eventually be exposed to the burning sun and will ask, "What is it that burns me?" He will be told, "It is the sun." "What? This sun that I hear lauded and admired every day: this is what torments me? May it be accursed!" And he detests this beautiful star because he does not see it, and not to see it will be his punishment. For if he were to see it, the sun itself would, with its kindly light, show him where he might seek cover from its burning rays. All of his misery, then, lies in not seeing it. But why should we speak of the sun, when after all it is nothing but a great lifeless body that we see only with our eyes? Let us speak of another light, always ready to shine in the depths of our soul and fill it with light. What happens to the willfully blind man who prevents it from shining for him? He is sunk into the shadows and made unhappy.

And you, O eternal light! You remain in your glory and your brilliance, and you manifest your grandeur such that no one loses you but that the loss is his own. Father of lights, you have given a similar character to your Christ, so as to make manifest that he is God as you are, the brilliance of your glory, the radiance of your light, the imprint of your substance. He is the downfall of some and the resurrection of others, and by his great brilliance he is a sign of contradiction, for whoever lacks the strength or the courage to see him, will necessarily blaspheme him.

O my God, what has happened to the head and the master will also happen to the members and the disciples. This proud world is not worthy to see the disciples and imitators of Jesus Christ, nor to know them. They must be disdained and contradicted, placed in the ranks of the mad, the outmoded, the feeble-minded, who put on a good show, but inside nourish themselves with glory and vanity like everyone else. What has the world not invented to throw against your humble servants? This is the way that you have desired to give them part of your character and of your Son's. Therefore, I wish to be hidden in you with Jesus Christ, until truth appears in triumph.

And you, whoever you may be, to whom Divine Providence should bring this book, be you great or small, poor or rich, wise or ignorant, priest or layman, monk or nun: go now to the foot of the altar and contemplate Jesus there, in the sacrament where he hides. Remain there in silence. Say nothing to him. Look upon him and wait for him to speak to you in the depths of your heart. You will see him. I have died, he says, and my life is hidden in God until I appear in my glory to judge the world. Hide yourself in God with me, and do not think of appearing until I appear. If you are alone, I will be your companion. If you are weak, I will be your strength. If you are poor, I will be your treasure. If you are hungry, I will be your food. If you are afflicted, I will be your consolation and your joy. If you are bored, I will be your delight. If you are falling, I will hold you up. "Behold, I stand at the door and knock; if any one hears my voice and opens the door, I will come in to him and eat with him, and he with me" (Rev. 3:20). I do not wish for a third: none other but you and me.

And I will give you "to eat of the tree of life, which is in the paradise of God," and the "hidden manna," the taste of which no one knows except him to whom it is given (Rev. 2:7, 17). "Let him who is thirsty come, let him who desires take the water of life without price" (Rev. 22:17). So may it be, O Lord, who live and reign with the Father and the Holy Spirit, world without end. Amen.

Week 4: Wednesday

God, the Life of the Soul

God did not make death. On the contrary, he created
the rational soul to dwell in indissoluble union with the
human body. When the psalmist sang, "A body hast thou
prepared for me" (Heb. 10:5; cf. Ps. 39:7, Douay-Rheims
[RSV = Ps. 40:7]), it was as if he had said to the Creator:
O Lord, you have made my soul of a nature different from
that of my body, for, after having formed this body from
mud, that is, from moist earth, it was neither from earth,
nor water, nor from a mixture of the moist and the dry, nor
finally from any matter at all that you drew forth the soul
that you have mixed into this mass to give it life. It was
from yourself, from your mouth that you brought it forth;
you breathed the "breath of life" (Gen. 2:7), and the man
was animated, not by the arrangement of his organs, not
by the harmony of the elements, but by a principle of
life that you brought forth from within yourself, by a new
creation, entirely different from the one by which you

had drawn forth the material world from nothingness. This is why when you wanted to make man, you began a new order of things, a new creation. "Let us make man" (Gen. 1:26); it was another work, another method, different from the one that preceded it and entirely unlike it.

God made this soul with an immortal nature. Setting aside the other arguments that show us this truth, it suffices to consider the one given to us by sacred Scripture. This is that God made man in his image, and his soul is a participation in the life of God. In a certain way the soul lives like him, because it lives by reason and intelligence, and God has made it capable of loving and knowing him as he loves and knows himself. This is why, being made in his image and bound to his immortal truth, the soul does not take her being from matter and is not subject to its laws. For this reason, the soul does not die, regardless of what change happens to the matter beneath her, unless the one who drew it forth and made it in his image were suddenly to loosen his grip and let it fall into the abyss.

Nevertheless, as the soul belongs to the lowest order of intelligent substances, it is the one to form the bond between spirits and bodies. God has made spiritual substances in different degrees of perfection; the lowest is so imperfect that its nature is to be united to a body. For everything is disposed in order, and the first Being gives being and diffuses himself according to that order. Thus the rational soul finds itself united to a body by its nature.

Yet the words "a body hast thou prepared for me" have a still more particular significance. For we can imagine the rational soul speaking to its Creator, saying: "At the same time as you made me to be immortal by creating me according to your image, you also prepared a body that suits me so well that our peace and our union would have been eternal and unbreakable had not sin, coming between us, troubled the heavenly harmony." How did sin disunite two things so well adjusted to one another? It may be understood by this teaching of St. Augustine: "It is an unchanging law of divine justice that the evil we choose should be punished by an evil we hate. It is, therefore, just that having chosen sin, death should follow, contrary to our will, and that our souls should be constrained to leave our bodies by the punishment of the one who abandoned God voluntarily."

It is in this way that "as sin came into the world," death, as the apostle says, came by the same means (Rom. 5:12). This is why the Son of God destroyed death only after having destroyed sin. And before speaking the word of resurrection to the dead at the end of time, he speaks the word of repentance to sinners now. Listen, you who are dead in spirit, Jesus Christ calls you to be reborn with him: "Why will you die, O house of Israel?" (Ezek. 33:11). Come forth from your tombs. Leave your bad habits behind.

"Truly, truly, I say to you, the hour is coming, and now is, when the dead will hear the voice of the Son of God, and those who hear will live" (John 5:25). The dead will hear the voice of the Son of God, both those dead in body and those dead in spirit. For as St. Augustine teaches us: "The soul is the life of the body, and God is the life of the soul." Just as the body dies when it loses its soul, so does the spirit die when it loses its God.

This death is one that cannot be sensed, and yet, if we knew how to see into things, if only we could understand how much more to be feared is the death of the soul due to sin, we would then willingly suffer the death of our bodies instead, even though that death seems so cruel to us. For if it is a great evil for the body to lose its soul, how much worse it is for the soul to lose its God! If we are seized with horror to see the cold and senseless body struck down, without power or movement, how much more horrible it is to contemplate the rational soul when separated from God: it is a spiritual cadaver that lives now only to make its death eternal. It is to those who are dead in spirit, to the souls of sinners, that Jesus Christ speaks, calling them to repent: "The hour is coming, and now is."

Week 4: Thursday

The Witness of the Baptist

"The baptism of John, whence was it?" (Matt. 21:25, Douay-Rheims). Is it possible that the Savior should rely upon the witness of St. John the Baptist? He was only his precursor; he was not the Bridegroom, but the friend of the Bridegroom. He was not the Christ, but the one sent to prepare his way, one who was not worthy to loosen the strap of his sandal. Jesus nevertheless relies upon his witness to convince those who were unwilling to believe the Christ himself. Yet John did not work a single miracle, while Jesus filled all of Judea with them. John spoke as a servant, while Jesus, as Son, told what he had seen in the bosom of the Father. "So weak are our eyes," says St. Augustine, "that a lamp suits them better than sunlight. We seek the sun by the light of a lamp." Jesus understood this point, saying, "The testimony which I have is greater than that of John" (John 5:36). When he made use of John's witness, therefore, it was to bring to our poor eyes a light more suited to their weakness. O profound blindness of men more willing to believe St. John than Jesus Christ himself! O God, who would not tremble? Who does not tremble to ask you the reason for this strange disposition of the hearts of the Jews? Is there not something similar in us?

"If we say, 'From heaven,' he will say to us, 'Why then did you not believe him?'" (Matt. 21:25). He had already told them, and they had not known how to respond: "You sent to John, and he has borne witness to the truth" (John 5:33). If they had admitted the heavenly mission of St. John the Baptist, he would have shut their mouths by his testimony. What then to say? "But if we say 'From men,' we are afraid of the multitude; for all hold that John was a prophet. So they answered Jesus 'We do not know.' And he said to them, 'Neither will I tell you by what authority I do these things'" (Matt. 21:26-27). Men of bad faith, who dare neither admit nor deny the mission of St. John the Baptist, you do not deserve a response from me. Admit, deny, think what you will: you are confounded, and there is nothing for you but to be silent. The other way was to believe in Jesus, but they could not, for reasons which would become clear in time.

Let us consider the whole passage from St. John's Gospel: "You sent to John, and he has borne witness to the truth. Not that the testimony which I receive is from man; but I say this that you may be saved. He was a burning and shining lamp, and you were willing to rejoice for a while in his light. But the testimony which I have is greater than that of John; for the works which the Father has granted me to accomplish, these very works which I am doing, bear me witness that the Father has sent me" (John 5:33-36).

This is what the witness of St. John the Baptist is for: so that you may be saved, so that you may yourselves be convinced. Thus are the pride and hypocrisy of the chief priests and elders revealed. They did not deserve that the Savior should say any more to them than they had already heard a hundred times and which those hundred times they had not believed. What will happen to us on the last day, when the truth, manifested in power, will eternally confront us in the sight of the whole universe? Where will we go? Where shall we hide?

Up to Jerusalem

The hour of Jesus approaches. He goes willingly to Jerusalem, where he knows he must die, and he declares it to his disciples.

St. Paul said to the elders of the church of Ephesus: "And now, bound in the Spirit," that is, gently constrained and inwardly pressed, "I am going to Jerusalem ... not knowing what shall befall me there" (Acts 20:22). But Jesus went to Jerusalem knowing full well what he had to suffer there and telling his Apostles: "Behold, we are going up to Jerusalem; and the Son of man will be delivered to the chief priests and scribes, and they will ... deliver him to the Gentiles" (Matt. 20:18-19). St. Paul, however, confessed his ignorance; all he knew was "that the Holy Spirit testifies to me in every city that imprisonment and afflictions await me" (Acts 20:23). Instead of revealing things in part, as he did to St. Paul, Jesus explained everything in full to his Apostles, as the Gospel confirms.

Up to Jerusalem

Although Jesus spoke plainly, the disciples "understood none of these things," for "this saying was hidden from them, and they did not grasp what was said" (Luke 18:34). By the care that he takes to show us the Apostles' ignorance, St. Luke wishes us to appreciate how difficult it was for them to understand the mystery of the Cross.

St. Luke elsewhere notes the Apostles' incomprehension: "They did not understand this saying, and it was concealed from them, that they should not perceive it; and they were afraid to ask him about this saying" (Luke 9:45). They did not understand because they did not want to understand. They saw clearly that they must follow their Master, and they did not want to know about the suffering that lay ahead for him, for fear of having a similar fate. This is why Jesus said to them: "Let these words sink into your ears; for the Son of man is to be delivered into the hands of men" (Luke 9:44). He took care to inculcate this truth during the time when everyone was admiring the miracles he worked. Flattered by his glory, their hearts were closed to what he taught them about the opprobrium he would have to suffer; they did not want to hear about it. Yet it was precisely this message that Jesus wanted them to understand. For in his suffering and in our obligation to follow him and to carry our cross after him is our salvation. "Let these words sink into your ears."

Consider how prone we are to self-deception, how we play deaf when we are told something that would injure our passions or sensibilities, and how, no matter how plainly we are spoken to, we stop our ears, pretending not to hear and fearing to understand what is said. "Leave this thing behind," "deny yourself this pleasure," "renounce your will": these things we do not hear. We do not want to hear them or know about them or ask for clarification about them. It is for this reason that St. Mark recounts the same episode in these terms: "They were on the road going up to Jerusalem, and Jesus was walking ahead of them; and they were amazed, and those who followed were afraid. And taking the Twelve again, he began to tell them what was to happen to him, saying, 'Behold, we are going up to Jerusalem'" (Mark 10:32-33). And he told them about all that he would suffer there.

The cause of their astonishment was that they knew that the scribes and Pharisees were seeking to put him to death, and that they could not comprehend his decision to place himself in their hands, and they followed him trembling. We fear to follow Jesus to the Cross.

But to encourage us, he walks ahead. St. Luke remarks that "he steadfastly set his face to go to Jerusalem" (Luke 9:51, Douay-Rheims). His human nature felt fear, as he showed us by his agony in the garden. For he willed to carry our weaknesses in order to teach us to overcome them. Let us follow him, and according to his example, let us steadfastly set our faces when we must go toward penance, mortification, and the Cross.

It was on this occasion that his disciples said to him: "Rabbi, the Jews were but now seeking to stone you, and are you going there again?" (John 11:8). They wanted to persuade him against the journey. Thomas alone understood the mystery, saying generously: "Let us also go, that we may die with him" (John 11:16). Noble words, had they been followed by the deed! Yet Thomas fled like the others, and he was the last to believe in the Resurrection. Such is man: the one who speaks the boldest is, often as not, shown to be the weakest when God abandons him to his own powers. Understand, Christian, how hard it is to go up to the Cross with Jesus and how great is our need for his grace.

No Man Ever Spoke Like This Man

Although we are very far away from that blessed vision in which we shall clearly see the Father in the Son and the Son in the Father, the Son of God comes to teach us that the Father has already begun to manifest himself in him in two marvelous ways: by his words and by the works of his might that are his miracles.

"Do you not believe that I am in the Father and the Father is in me? The words that I say to you I do not speak on my own authority" (John 14:10). If I am not from myself, I do not speak on my own authority; if I am the word, I am the word of someone. The one who makes me speak gives me my being, and all my words are from him, inasmuch as the substantial word from which are born all the words that I speak is from him.

The words of Jesus Christ have something divine about them, in their simplicity, in their profundity, and in the mild authority with which he speaks. "No man ever spoke like this man" (John 7:46). No man had ever enjoyed the natural authority over minds that belongs to the truth, which effortlessly and without the affectation of a lofty manner gives him a power over us that penetrates to the heart but is mild and peaceful.

Yet the marvel of these words is that a man who speaks as God at the same time speaks as one who receives everything from another: "What I say ... I say as the Father has bidden me" (John 12:50), and as he always bids me, because he speaks to me continually, for I am his word. "My teaching is not mine, but his who sent me" (John 7:16). And what proof of this does he give? "He who speaks on his own authority seeks his own glory; but he who seeks the glory of him who sent him is true, and in him there is no falsehood" (John 7:18).

My Savior, do not speak too much like a creature. What is a creature if not something that is not from itself, which has nothing of its own, which is always borrowing? The difference is immense between what is produced from all eternity and what is produced in time. The former exists forever; the latter does not exist forever and is able to cease existing. It is drawn forth from nothingness, and in itself is nothingness. What a great difference there is, consequently, between coming from God as his work and coming from God as his Son! One is created, the other begotten. One is drawn from nothingness and in itself is nothingness. The other is drawn from the substance of God and consequently is being itself.

My God, do I dare to follow this light? Man is father, but is he a true father? What does he give to his son? A man's son does share his nature; but was it the father who gave him that nature? No, certainly not. In what manner, then, did it come from him? Most imperfectly. True paternity is found in God, who, begetting his Son from his very being gave him his entire substance and made him not only his equal but one with him: "I and the Father are one" (John 10:30).

His Father, forever abundant, communicates to him all of his being, holding nothing back. It is one thing to lend, that is, to choose to give what one might not give, and it is another thing to abound. We need to attempt to understand the Father's abundance, fullness, fruitfulness, his full effusion of himself, remaining in himself to beget another like himself, who receives everything by being begotten, just as great, just as eternal, just as perfect as the Father. God does not come from God by being drawn forth from nothingness, but God comes from God by being drawn forth from his very substance. Producing another self would degrade him if he produced something less than himself. God, therefore, has come from God, the perfect Son from the perfect Father, perfectly one with him, because he receives his nature from him, and it is his nature to be one: "Hear, O Israel, the Lord our God is one" (Deut. 6:4).

Should we dare to peer into these profound depths? Why has Jesus Christ revealed it to us? Why does he return to the subject so often? When we stop to consider these truths, do we not risk forgetting the sublimity of Christian doctrine? We must tremble when we consider them. We must consider them through faith. We must, while listening to Jesus Christ and to these divine words, believe that they come from God, and believe at the same time that this God from whom they come himself comes from God and that he is Son. At each word that we hear, we must return all the way to the source and contemplate the Father in the Son and the Son in the Father.

Speak, then, speak O Jesus! Speak, you who are the word itself. I see you in your words because they make me see that you are God. But I also see your Father in them, because they teach me that you are God from God, the Word, and the Son of God (John 1:1, 14).

The Raising of Lazarus

Jesus nears Jerusalem. He is already at Bethany, a village at the foot of the Mount of Olives. His death nears, and what he does to prepare us for it is miraculous: He raises Lazarus from the dead.

Jesus was going up to Jerusalem to die, and it would seem that death's empire was stronger than ever once he had fallen under its power. But he works the great miracle of the raising of Lazarus to show us that he is death's master.

All of the terror of death is here before us. Lazarus is dead, enshrouded, entombed, and already decaying and putrid. They fear to move the stone covering his tomb lest they infect the place and loose its unbearable stench. Here is a horrid spectacle: Jesus shudders to see the tomb, and he weeps. In the death of his friend Lazarus he deplores the punishment shared by all men. He looks upon human nature as created for immortality, but condemned to death by sin. He is the friend of all mankind, and he comes to restore us. He commences by shedding a tear for our disaster and shuddering at the sight of the punishment that he himself will soon face for us. To him, what seems so awful about death is chiefly that it is caused by sin. It is sin, rather than death, that moves him to shudder, to be troubled in spirit, and to weep. He is all the more greatly moved as he draws near the tomb. This frightful cavern where the dead man has been laid: what can be done? "Could not he who opened the eyes of the blind man have kept this man from dying?" (John 11:37). They did not ask whether he could raise him because they could not imagine it to be possible. They thought that all Jesus could offer in the presence of this evil were his tears and sorrow. Here is all mankind in death: nothing is to be done except to lament its fate. No other resource is at hand. So does the story begin. The opening scene is one of desolation.

Yet the second is all consolation, for we see the power and victory of Jesus over death.

Jesus says, "This illness is not unto death; it is for the glory of God" (John 11:4). Yet Lazarus did in fact die; what the Savior meant is that death would here be vanquished and the Son of God glorified in the victory. He continued: "Lazarus has fallen asleep, but I go to awaken him out of sleep" (John 11:11), calling his death a falling asleep and showing that it is as easy for him to raise the dead as to awaken a sleeper.

As he approaches, he is progressively revealed to be the victor over death. "If you had been here," Martha says, "my brother would not have died. And even now I know that whatever you ask from God, God will give you" (John 11:21-22). You are all-powerful, not only to prevent death, but also to wrest its prey from its grasp. "Your brother will rise again." "I know that he will," says Martha, "on the last day" (cf. John 11:23-24). She does not doubt that Jesus can resurrect him before then, but she does not think herself worthy of that grace.

Let us savor the words of Jesus to Martha, after which death has no sting: "I am the resurrection and the life; he who believes in me, though he die, yet shall he live, and whoever lives and believes in me shall never die" (John 11:25-26). He will never die. Death for him will be only a journey. He will not remain there, and he will arrive at a condition in which he will never die. Martha's faith is great. In her spirit she sees the general resurrection and confesses Jesus Christ as the One who, being in Heaven and in the Father's bosom, is come into the world. Jesus, Son of the living God, lives with the same life as his Father. "As the Father has life in himself," he says, "so he has granted the Son also to have life in himself" (John 5:26). It is with good reason, then, that he tells us that he is "the resurrection and the life" and "as the Father raises the dead and gives them life, so also the Son gives life to whom he will" (John 5:21). He is a source of life; he is the same life as the Father. Life came to us when he became man. "We proclaim to you," says St. John, "the eternal life which was with the Father and was made manifest to us" (1 John 1:2).

"Father, I know that thou hearest me always" (John 11:42, Douay-Rheims). Thus are we delivered, for such an intercessor speaks on our behalf. "Lazarus, come out." The prophets had raised several men from the dead, but none of them had treated death in such an imperious manner. It was, as the Savior said, the hour "when the dead will hear the voice of the Son of God, and those who hear will live" (John 5:25). What is done now for Lazarus alone, one day will be done for all men.

It is important that we meditate upon these words and deeds so that we may be strengthened against the fear of death, which is so extreme in us that it is capable of making men lose their minds. We must arm ourselves against this fear, chiefly by meditating upon the promises of the Gospel and attaching ourselves with a living faith to the truth that Jesus has vanquished death. He did so in the case of a young girl still in her bed, a widow's son being carried on a bier, and in the person of Lazarus. These three to whom he restored life remained mortal. What was left for him to do was to vanquish mortality itself. It was in his own person that he would win so perfect a victory. After he had been put to death, he rose, never to die again, and without having first seen corruption, as the psalmist sings: "Thou wilt not let thy holy one see corruption" (Ps. 15:10, Douay-Rheims [RSV = Ps. 16:10]). What was done in the head will be accomplished in the members. Immortality has been assured to us by Jesus Christ.

Judge Not

"Judge not" (Matt. 7:1). There is a Judge above you, who will judge your judgments, who will demand of you an accounting of them, who will punish you for judging without authority and without understanding.

Without authority. "Who are you to pass judgment on the servant of another? It is before his own master that he stands or falls" (Rom. 14:4). It belongs to the master to judge. Do not judge those whose judge you are not. St. Paul continues: "Why do you pass judgment on your brother? Or you, why do you despise your brother?" (Rom. 14:10). He is your brother, your equal: it does not belong to you to judge him. You are both subject to the judgment of the great judge before whom all men must appear: "We shall all stand before the judgment seat of God," and "each of us shall give account of himself to God" (Romans 14:10, 12). Do not think at all about what others do; think instead about the account you must render of yourself.

St. James is no less forceful. "There is one lawgiver and judge ... who is able to save and to destroy." For this reason he then asks, "Who are you that you judge your neighbor?" (James 4:12). He has derived this truth from this beautiful principle: "He that speaks evil against a brother or judges his brother, speaks evil against the law and judges the law" (James 4:11). For the law prohibits you from making this judgment. "But if you judge the law," the apostle continues, "you are not a doer of the law but a judge." You raise yourself above your measure, and the law will soon fall upon you with all of its weight, and you will be crushed by it. See with how much force the light of truth is ranged against your presumptuous judgments in these two verses.

You see that you lack proper authority to judge; now see that you also judge without understanding. You do not know the one whom you judge. You do not see into the interior. You do not know his intentions, which may perhaps justify him. And if his crime is manifest, you do not know whether he will one day repent, or whether he has already repented, or whether he is one of those whose conversions will cause great rejoicing in Heaven. Therefore do not judge.

Charity is not suspicious and does not think ill of others. Charity is mild, "patient and kind," "bears all things,

believes all things, hopes all things, endures all things."
She does not "rejoice at wrong," but rejoices when everyone pursues the good in truth (1 Cor. 13:4-7). Charity,
therefore, does not take pleasure in judging.

Much more than she judges others, charity judges and
condemns herself. "You have no excuse, O man, whoever
you are, when you judge another; for in passing judgment
upon him you condemn yourself, because you, the judge,
are doing the very same things" (Rom. 2:1). You judge
yourself by your own mouth, and you pronounce your
own sentence. "For with the judgment you pronounce
you will be judged, and the measure you give will be the
measure you get" (Matt. 7:2).

If at the end of our life we would hear, "You will not be
judged" (cf. Matt. 7:1), we must judge not.

Week 5: Tuesday

The Pharisees

The Savior's reign should be glorious and brilliant, although with a different glory and brilliance than the carnal Jews had imagined. Jesus showed them that nothing was easier than for him to be recognized by the people as their king. It was necessary, however, that there be contradiction in his triumph, and this we see in the jealousy of the chief priests, the scribes, and the Pharisees. Their jealousy is explained by St. John. While everyone else flocked to see the Savior and to praise him, the Pharisees said among themselves: "You see that you can do nothing; look, the world has gone after him" (John 12:19). This they could not endure.

They were eaten up by jealousy. While even the children were crying out that he was the son of David, they said to him: "Teacher, rebuke your disciples" (Luke 19:39); "Do you hear what these are saying?" (Matt. 21:16). Jesus said two things in reply. First: "Have you never read, 'Out of the mouths of babes and sucklings thou has brought perfect praise'?" (Matt. 21:16, Douay-Rheims). Should you be surprised if children offer praise to God in my person? If you had the simplicity and sincerity of innocent youth, you would praise God as they do; like them you would honor the One whom he sends. But your envy, vainglory, hypocrisy, and machinations prevent you. Strip yourselves of these vices and clothe yourselves with the innocence and simplicity of children, that you may sing the praises of Jesus Christ with sincerity and purity.

The Savior's second response to the Pharisees was to say: "I tell you, if these were silent, the very stones would cry out" (Luke 19:40). For God is sufficiently powerful, as St. John the Baptist explained, "from these stones to raise up children to Abraham" (Matt. 3:9), and from the most hardened of hearts to make true believers. The time was to come, and has come, when the glory of Jesus Christ would ring out so loudly throughout the earth that the nations would assemble at the sound, and God would be worshipped by a people who had hitherto not known him and who had been sound asleep in their sins. O stones, O hardened hearts: you must awaken at these words of the Savior!

While the people applauded the Savior and made his praises mount to Heaven, his enemies, not content that their boundless envy should appear only in their speech, made secret plans to kill him.

Let us contemplate the effects of jealousy, which is one of the most severe wounds upon our nature. Jesus, who came to heal us of it, first had to feel all of its malice, and the suffering that envy would cause him was to serve as that venom's remedy. Envy is the black and secretive effect of a weak pride, which feels itself diminished by the very least achievements of others. It is the most dangerous poison of our self-love, which begins by consuming the one who vomits it forth upon others and leads him to commit deeds most vile. For pride is naturally enterprising and wants to shine, but envy hides itself under all sorts of pretexts and is pleased by secretive and dark ways. Hidden lies, calumny, treason: every evil trick is its portion and cup. It shines forth, and brings forward against the just man—whose good reputation confronts its—every insult and mockery, with all the bitterness of hatred and the last excesses of cruelty. O Savior! O Just One! O Holy of holies! This is what had to be accomplished upon your person.

Let us tear out the splinters of envy lodged deep in our hearts. Let us consider the malice and the horror of such a poison.

Week 5: Wednesday

The Scribes

While he was preaching in the Temple, "the chief priests and the scribes with the elders came up and said to him, 'Tell us by what authority you do these things'" (Luke 20:1-2). While they seemed to be asking chiefly about his authority to teach, the question extended to everything else that Jesus had done. It was as if they had asked him: "By what authority do you enter so solemnly into the Temple? By what authority do you teach? In the name of what power do you chase off the money changers? Only we can give you that authority, but we have not given it to you. Whence does it come?" These are questions that the scribes and priests have a right to ask. Jesus, however, does not give them any instruction on this point: "Neither will I tell you by what authority I do these things" (Luke 20:8). Instead, he reveals their bad faith and hypocrisy.

Jesus is so easily understood by those with docile and humble spirits! The Samaritan woman, a sinner, speaks openly to him about the Christ, and he says to her directly: "I who speak to you am he" (John 4:26). "Do you believe in the Son of man?" he asks the man born blind. "Who is he, sir, that I may believe in him?" "You have seen him, and it is he who speaks to you." "Lord, I believe," and he adored him (John 9:35-38). So it is in other places. When he does not respond in this straightforward manner, which is so fitting, it is because the men to whom he is speaking are not worthy.

"By what authority are you doing these things?" (Matt. 21:23). He had already answered them in a similar case. Having said to a paralytic, "Take heart, my son; your sins are forgiven" (Matt. 9:2), which was to do something much greater than he had ever done, and the scribes finding this to be strange, he spoke to them in this way: "Which is easier, to say, 'Your sins are forgiven,' or to say, 'Rise and walk'? But that you may know that the Son of man has authority on earth to forgive sins," he said to the man, "Rise, take up your bed and go home" (Matt. 9:5-6). He had, therefore, clearly established his power to forgive sins, which is the greatest power that could be given to a man. There was nothing more to ask him; the only thing to do was to submit. As they could not resolve to do so, they came to him again: "By what authority do you do these things?" (cf. Luke 20:2), as if they had said, "By what power do you heal the sick?" "By what power do you restore sight to the blind?" "By what power do you raise the dead?" It was only too clear that he did these things by the power of God, and only an evil spirit could have prompted them to ask him about matters so evident.

Elsewhere in the same spirit they ask him, "How long will you keep us in suspense? If you are the Christ, tell us plainly" (John 10:24). To hear them speak so forcibly, you would think that they were in good faith and wanted to know the truth, but the response of Jesus shows that the contrary was the case. You want me to tell you openly who I am, but "I told you, and you do not believe. The works that I do in my Father's name, they bear witness to me" (John 10:25). They had two witnesses: his word and, what was even stronger, his miracles. The eternal truth, which they poorly consulted, had nothing more to say to them and nothing more to do than to confound them before the people. And we come to the same impasse when we question our own conscience about matters that are already plainly resolved: we are only seeking to trick the world or to trick ourselves. Let us cease to flatter ourselves. Let us stop seeking the expedients that will bring about our ruin. Let us break this dangerous and scandalous commerce by giving back the good we have wrongly acquired. Let us be faithful to the duties of our profession. Let us not retreat before the precepts of the Gospel, and let us certainly not seek the broad way that leads to perdition.

Jesus Is Persecuted

The calumny of the scribes and Pharisees should prompt us to reflect upon the injustice of man. They admired Jesus and realized that they were unable to "catch him by what he said," neither before Pontius Pilate nor before the people (Luke 20:26). Did they then convert or stop trying to murder him? On the contrary, the more convinced they became and the less they were able to oppose him with reasons, the more they became enraged against him.

They appeared to be zealous for the liberty of the people of God and against the idolatrous empire, inasmuch as they asked his advice about the taxes due to Rome. Yet these same men who showed this false zeal would three days later cry out to Pilate: "If you release this man, you are not Caesar's friend" (John 19:12). Still worse was what one of his chief accusers said: "We found this man perverting our nation, and forbidding us to give tribute to

Caesar" (Luke 23:2). The very contrary was the truth, as Jesus had made clear.

What could prevent calumny, if plain speech had failed to do so? All that Jesus could do now was to endure what God allowed to befall him and be content knowing his own innocence.

Let us plumb the depths of the human heart and take the measure of its injustice. The same men who here pretend to be zealous against the idolatrous empire will have recourse to it against Jesus and even invoke it against his disciples. If the support of the people is needed, Caesar is their foe. If they need him to murder their enemy, Caesar is their friend. Men judge what is just according to their passions, calling things good which satisfy them and even making use of political power to appease their passions, when its real purpose is to curb them.

"Render to Caesar the things that are Caesar's, and to God the things that are God's" (Luke 20:25). Never has a response been more to the point than this one. No lesson was more necessary for the Jewish people then, stirred up as they were with the spirit of revolt that burst out shortly afterward to their ruin. The Pharisees and the zealots secretly encouraged this evil tendency. But Jesus, always full of grace and truth, did not wish to leave the world without having taught them what they owed to their prince and without warning them against a rebellion that would bring ruin upon their nation.

He also knew that his followers would be persecuted by the Caesars, whose very name and authority would soon intervene in the punishment being prepared for him. Jesus was not unaware of it; he had already predicted it. "The Son of man," he said, would be delivered "to the Gentiles to be mocked and scourged and crucified" (Luke 20:18-19). He also knew that the same treatment awaited the Apostles and that the Jews would "deliver [them] up" and that they would "be dragged before governors and kings" (Matt. 10:19, 18) out of hatred for his gospel.

Although he knew all these things, he was just toward the princes his persecutors, upholding the authority by which they would oppress him and his Church. And he taught his disciples to submit to those in power, and to do so meekly and without bitterness. "When he suffered," St. Peter says, "he did not threaten; but he trusted to him who judges justly" (1 Pet. 2:23).

Let us never complain, even when we think ourselves to have been unjustly oppressed. But let us imitate our Savior, and preserving what is God's — the purity of our conscience — let us with willing hearts render what is due to all men, even to unjust judges, should the case arise, or even to our greatest enemies. What we ought to do when they have wronged us, with much greater reason ought we to do when they have not and when it is our passion alone that makes us complain.

Week 5: Friday

The True Messiah

"These know that thou hast sent me" (John 17:25, Douay-Rheims). They "know in truth that I came from thee" (John 17:8, Douay-Rheims). Happy are they whose faith is acknowledged by Jesus! Let us examine ourselves with respect to this important disposition of the heart. Let us listen to St. Paul: "Examine yourselves, to see whether you are holding to your faith. Test yourselves" (2 Cor. 13:5). See how he presses us, how he inculcates this duty: "Examine yourselves. Test yourselves." Do you believe with perfect certitude that Jesus Christ was truly sent by God? What reason could you have not to believe? Have you not seen in him all of the marks that the prophets and patriarchs ascribed to the Messiah? Did he not work all the miracles he needed to work and in every circumstance in which they were necessary, as sure testimony that he was the one who was to come, the one truly sent from God?

Has anyone else ever taught a doctrine so holy, so pure, so perfect that he has been able to say, like Jesus, "I am the light of the world" (John 8:12)? Where will you find more charity toward men, more holy deeds, a more beautiful model of perfection, a milder authority, greater condescension toward us poor sinners, even to the extent of making himself our advocate, intercessor, and victim? This is what he explains in these words we so love: "Come to me, all who labor and are heavy laden, and I will give you rest. Take my yoke upon you, and learn from me; for I am gentle and lowly in heart, and you will find rest for your souls. For my yoke is easy, and my burden is light" (Matt. 11:28-30). Man needs to have a yoke, a law, an authority, a commandment; otherwise, carried away by his passions, he will lose his self-control. Everything that we could wish for is here: to find a master like Jesus, who knows how to make constraint mild and burdens light. Where shall we find consolation, encouragement, and the words of eternal life if we do not find them in him? Do you believe all this? This is the first part of our examination of conscience.

When we have said, "Yes, I believe it, I recognize it with that 'full assurance of faith' of which St. Paul speaks [Heb. 10:22], with 'full conviction' [1 Thess. 1:5]," then St. John will say to us: "By this we may be sure that we know him, if we keep his commandments. He who says 'I know him' but disobeys his commandments is a liar, and the truth is not in him." And, a little while later, "He who says he abides in him ought to walk in the same way in which he walked" (1 John 2:3-4, 6) and follow his example. Most certainly—for St. Paul said it—there are those who "profess to know God, but they deny him by their deeds" (Titus 1:16). And St. John said, "Little children, let us not love in word or speech but in deed and in truth" (1 John 3:18). Are we or are we not one of those who thus love? What account shall we have to give of our deeds? This is the second and more essential part of our examination of conscience.

The third part is the most important of all. "Beloved, if our hearts do not condemn us, we have confidence before God" (1 John 3:21). If we labor to live in such a way that we are sons and daughters of the truth, and we can persuade our heart of this in the presence of God, then we ought to believe that this is a gift of God, in conformity with the apostle's wish: "Peace be to the brethren, and love with faith, from God the Father and the Lord Jesus Christ" (Eph. 6:23). Should we enjoy this peace, we must take no glory for ourselves, but instead humble ourselves exceedingly, for all that we have brought to this our slipshod beginning of good works is wretchedness, poverty, and corruption. If we are lost when we stray from the path of virtue, how much more lost should we be were we to presume to climb it by our own strength?

After this, all that remains is to confess our sins, not with discouragement and despair, but with sweet hope, because the same St. John said, "If we confess our sins, he is faithful and just, and will forgive our sins and cleanse us from all unrighteousness" (1 John 1:9). Note it well: faithful and just. Not because he owes us anything, but because he has promised us everything in Jesus Christ. We can hope for pardon and his grace if we believe that he has sent Jesus Christ, who by his blood is "the expiation for our sins" (1 John 2:2).

A Sign of Contradiction

The holy prophet Simeon spoke truly when he told the Blessed Virgin, "This child is set for the fall and for the resurrection of many in Israel, and for a sign which shall be contradicted ... that, out of many hearts, thoughts may be revealed" (Luke 2:34-35, Douay-Rheims). At that moment, the profound malice of the human heart had not yet been seen, nor the extent to which it is capable of resisting God.

It should not astonish us that many believed in Jesus after the raising of Lazarus. The miracle had taken place in full view, at the very door of Jerusalem, with the crowd that the mourning of a family of good standing normally attracts. "Many of the Jews therefore ... believed in him" (John 11:45). It was the foreseeable effect of so great a miracle.

But others, knowing that the chief priests and the Pharisees hated Jesus, went to tell them what they had seen. Upon hearing the news, a council was assembled and came to a strange determination.

"This man performs many signs." They did not deny the fact, for it was too well attested. "What are we to do?" (John 11:47). The response would seem plain: to believe in him. But their avarice, false zeal, hypocrisy, ambition, and tyranny over consciences—faults which Jesus revealed, even though they were hidden under the mask of piety—these faults blinded them. In this condition, "they could not believe" (John 12:39). They would rather resist God than renounce their power.

Later they would say of the disciples: "What shall we do with these men? For that a notable sign has been performed through them is manifest to all the inhabitants of Jerusalem, and we cannot deny it" (Acts 4:16). The natural response would have been: we must believe in it. But if we believe in it, we will lose our standing. This they could not resolve to do.

The incredulous among us ask how was it that the whole world did not believe in him if he worked so many great miracles? They do not understand the profound attachment of the human heart to its senses, which brings a prodigious indifference to salvation. These attachments cause us to be complacent, to ignore things that pertain to our salvation, and to deafen ourselves to the claims of those that we do see, for fear of the consequences of belief. We fear having to renounce all that we love and embrace a life that seems so unbearable and sad.

In order to change the evil dispositions of our hearts, there must be internal miracles in addition to external ones. This is what grace achieves. There ought to be nothing easier than to discover the truth. But only a relatively small number of men desired the truth and their salvation enough to inquire into the things happening in Judea and to reflect upon them freely, that is, without attachment to their senses.

What is the more astonishing is that these men who did not see the will of God in the miracles that had so evidently declared it were held to be wise: the chief priests, the scribes, and the Pharisees. Yet they were hypocrites, who employed the name of God to mislead the world. They were proud, grasping men who made religion serve their interests. They were, therefore, opposed to the truth and incapable of accepting it. This is why Simeon said that by Christ the "thoughts out of many hearts [would] be revealed" (Luke 2:35); many would choose to follow those who appeared to be wise and who enjoyed high standing rather than to follow God and the truth.

Far from profiting from the miracle of the resurrection of Lazarus, they resolved to kill not only Jesus, but Lazarus as well (John 11:53 and 12:10). Too many people were going to see him; his witness against them was too strong. They thought they would be able to hide the miracle of his being raised by showing that the Savior had not been able to keep him alive for long. They planned to kill him, as if they could thereby tie God's hands.

The blindness of the Jews is not so different from that of unbelievers today. The effort of self-mastery that must be made in order to give ourselves fully to the truth and to God is so great that many prefer to stifle the grace and inspiration that would lead them to make it. Many, that is, prefer blindness to sight. We are also among those to whom Jesus Christ is a sign of contradiction. One of the revelations of Christ's coming is the tremendous insensibility of those raised in the faith and surrounded by its light who nevertheless prefer their senses and the enchantment of pleasure to the truth that shines in their heart.

Palm Sunday

The Entry of
Our Lord into Jerusalem

Although the advent of Christ had to be accomplished in humility, contrary to the expectation of the Jews, it would not be utterly destitute of glory and brilliance. This brilliance was necessary so that the Jews might see that as humble as their Savior was, and as contemptible as he appeared, he could yet attract the greatest glory that men were capable of giving—even to the point of his being made king—had not the ingratitude of the Jews and a secret dispensation of God's wisdom prevented it.

This is what we see in his entry into Jerusalem, the most striking and beautiful royal entry ever made. A man who seems to be the lowliest in consideration and power, receives from all the people, both in the royal city and in the Temple, honors greater than any ever given to a king. This is the brilliance. Yet we must not forget the humility and infirmity that were inseparable from the earthly condition of the Son of God, and we will see them too, after we have considered his glory.

Although the Son of God appeared to be the least of men, he was born to be a king in the most admirable way possible. Because they admired his deeds, his holy life, his miracles—so compassionate toward mankind—the crowds had left everything to follow him, together with their wives and children, even into the desert lands far from their homes, without so much as thinking of their everyday needs. And when Jesus had fed them with five loaves and two fish, to the number of five thousand men "besides women and children" (Matt. 14:21), they were so amazed that they "were about to come and take him by force to make him king" and recognize him as the Christ (John 6:15). Visible then was some of the same brilliance that we see here today, in his entry into Jerusalem.

On the day of the Palms, however, it pleased him to allow his people's admiration to declare itself. This is why they ran before him with palms in their hands, crying out that he was their king, the true son of David who was to come, and the Messiah for whom they had waited. Children joined in, and their innocent witness shows us just how sincere was the people's joy. Never had so much been done for any king. The people cast their own clothing upon the path before him; they hewed down green branches to cover the road; everything, even the trees, seemed to bow before him. The costliest of tapestries ever displayed for a royal entry could not equal these simple, natural ornaments. The trees pruned and the people stripping themselves to prepare the way for their King: it was a ravishing spectacle. In other royal entries, the people are told to prepare the way, and their joy is, as it were, by command. Here everything was done by the movement of the people's hearts alone. No outward splendor struck the eye. This poor, meek King sat upon a donkey, a lowly, peaceful steed. There was no horse whose spiritedness would attract regard. There were neither followers nor guards, neither spoils of victory nor captive kings. The palms carried before him were the mark of another sort of victory. All of the apparatus of an ordinary triumph was banished from this one. In its place, we see the sick whom he had cured and the dead he had brought back to life. The person of the King and the memory of his miracles were what made the feast. All that art and flattery can design to honor a conqueror in a day of victory gave way before the simplicity and the truth that made their appearance here. With this holy festivity, they led the Savior to the middle of Jerusalem, to the holy mountain of the Temple. There he appeared as its lord and master, as the son of the royal house, the Son of the God who was worshipped there. Neither Solomon, its founder, nor the high priests who officiated there had ever received equal honors.

We should pause here and take the time to reflect upon the whole of this great spectacle.

Monday of Holy Week

The Anointing

As his time drew near, Jesus came forth from his retreat at Ephraim and returned to Bethany, to the neighborhood of Jerusalem, just six days before the Passover. He came for a feast at the house of his friend Lazarus. Martha was serving, as she usually did, while Mary observed the custom of the Jews and "took a pound of costly ointment of pure nard and anointed the feet of Jesus and wiped his feet with her hair," with the result that "the house was filled with the fragrance of the ointment" (John 12:3).

To anoint Jesus with a fragrant balm is to praise him. To anoint his head is to praise and adore his divinity, for "the head of Christ," as St. Paul says, "is God" (1 Cor. 11:3). To anoint his feet is to adore his humanity and its weakness. To wipe his feet with her hair was to place all her beauty and vanity beneath his feet. Thus did she sacrifice all to Jesus. Him alone she wished to please. How could the hair that had touched the feet of Jesus ever be put to the service of vanity again? This is how Jesus wants to be loved. He alone is worthy of such love, of such homage.

We must note that this profusion of oil scandalized the hypocrite and served as a pretext for him to condemn this woman's piety and accuse her of indiscretion. Judas did so to hide his envy of Jesus and of the honors paid to him and thus showed that he belongs in the company of those who are falsely charitable and falsely devout. The most wicked men are the most severe censors of the conduct of others, whether because of the disorder of their minds, or their hypocrisy, or their false zeal. Judas had yet another reason, which was that he kept the box that held what was given to the Savior and "used to take what was put into it" (John 12:6). How loudly avarice speaks when it covers itself with the pretext of charity!

His insolent words not only attacked Mary, but Jesus as well. Yet the Savior defended her, saying: "Let her alone, let her keep it for the day of my burial" (John 6:7). He considered himself as one already dead on account of the hour that was approaching, and he had put himself in the mind and the condition of a victim.

At the same time, he wanted us to consider how we could adequately honor his pure body, formed by the Holy Spirit, where dwelt Divinity itself, by which death would be conquered and the reign of sin abolished. What oil could ever be sufficiently fine to honor his purity? He also wanted the oil that might have served softness and luxury to serve piety, so that vanity would be thus sacrificed to truth.

To Judas's feigned concern that the oil had not been used in service of the poor, Jesus replied, "You always have the poor with you, and whenever you will, you can do good to them," but "you will not always have me" (Mark 14:7). Jesus must be served while his time remained, and then, after his departure, be consoled by our service to the poor, whose care he accepts as if it is given to him. How dear the poor ought to be to us, for they hold the place of Christ! Let us kiss their feet. Let us take part in their humiliations and their weakness. Let us lament their misery and suffer together with them. Let us pour out oil upon their feet as a consolation for their pain and a balm for their sorrow. Let us wipe them with our hair by sharing our abundance, and let us deprive ourselves of adornment that we might care for them.

At the same time, let us anoint Jesus. Let us breathe out from our hearts tender desire, chaste love, sweet hope, continual praise. If we wish to love and praise him worthily, let us praise him by our entire life; let us keep his word. Let us open our hearts to him and say with St.

Paul that he is "our wisdom, our righteousness and sanctification and redemption" (1 Cor. 1:30). Let us sing to him the sweet songs of the people he has redeemed: "Worthy is the Lamb who was slain, to receive power and wealth and wisdom and might and honor and glory and blessing!" (Rev. 5:12). This is what every creature ought to sing to him; this is the costly oil of anointing that we should pour forth from our hearts.

Tuesday of Holy Week

The Betrayal

"When Jesus had thus spoken, he was troubled in spirit," and he confessed it, saying: "One of you will betray me" (John 13:21).

This trouble in the holy soul and spirit of Jesus deserves careful attention. What we first notice is its cause: "one of you will betray me." The treason of one of his disciples causes Jesus this interior trouble. What troubles him in general, then, is sin, and especially the sins of those who were most closely united to him, like Judas, whom he had placed in the ranks of his Apostles. His Passion—by which he would destroy sin—would be the occasion for so many new crimes, enormous and unprecedented crimes such as the treason of Judas, the inhumanity and ingratitude of the Jews, and, in a word, deicide. It was the thought of these crimes that brought him such interior trouble and made some of the bitterest dregs of the chalice he had to drink.

There are three principal places where St. John speaks of the trouble Jesus felt in his holy soul: here, and in the previous chapter, when he said, "Now is my soul troubled" (John 12:27), and earlier when he saw the tears of Mary, who wept for the death of her brother Lazarus: "When Jesus saw her weeping, and the Jews who came with her also weeping, he was deeply moved in spirit and troubled" (John 11:33).

There is no doubt that at this moment the cause of his being troubled was the crime of Judas and of all those who would cooperate in his death. We may also see that when he said, "Now is my soul troubled" on the eve of his Passion, he was also chiefly thinking of this betrayal, for sin alone could cause him to be so moved. If he appeared so troubled at the death of Lazarus and by the tears shed on his behalf, we must not think that it was the death of Lazarus's body that caused him to shudder. It was, instead, the death of the soul that he saw, as in an image, in the death of the body, for he knew that it was sin that had brought death into the world. Lazarus was the image of a sinner, and of a sinner in the most deadly and frightful condition, which is when, by hardened and habitual sin, he rots in his crime.

The trouble that Jesus here feels in his soul is the horror that affects him when considering sin, which is what causes the internal suffering that manifests itself as a shudder. If we may be allowed to peer into his most intimate feelings, what caused him the greatest pain on this occasion was that he saw the evil effect that his death would produce in sinners, by being for them an occasion to abandon themselves to sin through the hope that his merits would obtain pardon for them. This is what is most horrid in sin, when God's goodness and the grace of redemption are put in its service. If this is what is most horrid about sin, it is also, consequently, what brought the Savior his greatest horror, his deepest shudders, and his troubled spirit.

The trouble that he felt at the approach of his death was not only caused by the perfidy that would result in his terrible death, but by its deeper causes. He had omitted nothing from his attempt to correct the Jews; their malice was the sole cause of their fury. It was also true that Jesus' holiness, his doctrine and miracles, and his insistent calls for their repentance all should have worked to their salvation; instead they excited jealousy and implacable hatred. Judas himself took the words that Jesus spoke in defense of Mary's anointing of his feet as the very occasion to leave him.

Jesus had to suffer death as the just punishment of all the sins whose weight he bore, in a certain sense as one guilty. Thus the horror of sin took hold of him. He saw himself surrounded by it and even penetrated by it. What a cruel spectacle for the Savior of mankind! He saw sin increase by the ill use to which his death would be put. It would make many say that he was not the Son of God and that all of his miracles had been so many illusions. It was scandal to the Jews, folly to the Greeks, and even at times to the faithful themselves. What an occasion of vengeance: for all those who would not profit from his death would become only more guilty, more worthy of punishment, and more subject to damnation. How touched by their misery was this good Savior, who so tenderly loves all men and who became man only to save us! O Jesus! This is what troubled your holy soul. This is what caused you to be moved. Let us then be horrified by sin, and let us see, in the troubles of Jesus, how greatly troubled our own conscience should be.

Wednesday of Holy Week

Washed of Our Sins

In the warmer regions of the East, bathing was frequent, and after one had washed in the morning and then again during the day, all that remained for the evening was to wash the feet so that the grime of one's comings and goings could be cleansed. This is the sense in which we are to take the words of the Spouse in the Song of Songs: "I had bathed my feet, how could I soil them?" (Song 5:3).

Jesus makes use of this image to teach his followers that after they have been washed of their greater sins, they still need to take care to purify themselves of those small sins they commit during the normal course of life. A soul that loves God never finds anything that offends him to be minor. If we neglect to purify ourselves of these faults, they will place our soul in a deadly state, imperceptibly weakening its powers in such a way that little strength will remain to resist great temptations, which can be defeated only by very ardent charity. "He who has bathed does not need to wash, except for his feet, but he is clean all over; and you are clean, but not all of you" (John 13:10). By these words, Jesus teaches us that we are not permitted to neglect lesser sins, for this is what he wished to signify by the washing of feet.

In order to peer deeper into this mystery, we should see that the care he takes to wash the feet of the Apostles at the moment when he is about to institute the Eucharist teaches us that the time when we ought to purge ourselves of our venial sins is when we are preparing for Communion, that most perfect union with Jesus Christ. To this union our sins are so great an obstacle that if we were to die before having expiated them, the Beatific Vision would be delayed, perhaps for centuries. We ought then to feel all the more obliged to purify ourselves of these sins before Communion, because it is by Communion that they are chiefly removed, the greater ones having been removed by the sacrament of Penance.

Neglect of these faults can proceed to such an excess that not only does our attachment to these sins become dangerous—which it always is—but even mortal. For the one who cares only about the sins that would damn him shows that it is punishment alone that he fears and that he does not truly love justice, that is to say, he does not love God as he is obliged to do. Such a one should fear to lose what remains to him of the divine fire of charity.

Let us then carefully wash ourselves, not only our hands and our head, but also our feet, before approaching the Eucharist. Jesus teaches his Apostles the seriousness of this obligation when he says to them, "If I do not wash you, you have no part in me" (John 13:8). This is not only because our sins retard the beatific vision and our perfect union with God, but because to neglect to wash them may bring a dangerous chill between our soul and Christ, and even become deadly.

Wash yourself, Christian, wash yourself of all your sins, even the least of them, when you are about to approach the holy table. Wash your feet with care. Renew yourself entirely, lest you eat the body of the Savior unworthily. Even when we are not completely unworthy — with that indignity that renders us unworthy of the Body and Blood of the Savior — we may still be unworthy to receive great graces, without which we cannot overcome great weaknesses, nor the great temptations of which life is full.

Lord, wash my feet, so that I can say with the Spouse, "I have bathed my feet, how could I soil them?" Purity is a magnet for attracting purity: the whiter one's clothing, the more noticeable are the stains upon it. The cleaner one is, the more one should avoid becoming soiled. Let us desire to be counted among those of whom it is written that they are "spotless" before the throne of God (Rev. 14:5). To this goal we should aspire, remembering the lovely teaching of St. Augustine that although we cannot live here below without sin, we can leave this life without sin, because while our sins are many, the remedies for healing them are not wanting.

Holy Thursday

The Eucharist

Let us read the words of the institution of the Eucharist at the Last Supper in St. Matthew's Gospel (26:26-28), adding the words of the other sacred authors on the same subject:

> Now as they were eating, Jesus took bread, and blessed, *and when he had given thanks* (1 Cor. 11:24), broke it, and gave it to the disciples and said, "Take, eat; this is my body, *which is given for you. Do this in remembrance of me*" (Luke 22:19).
>
> And he took a cup *after supper* (Luke 22:20), and when he had given thanks he gave it to them, saying, "Drink of it, all of you; for this is my blood of the *new covenant* (Luke 22:20), which is poured out for many for the forgiveness of sins. *Do this, as often as you drink it, in remembrance of me*" (1 Cor. 11:25).

Here is all that we have about the institution, other than that in place of St. Luke's "given for you," St. Paul has him say "broken for you" (1 Cor. 11:24 in certain ancient texts). The sense of each is the same. He was handed over to death, struck by blows, pierced with wounds, violently hung from a cross: he was broken. This is the body that Jesus gives to us, the same body that was about to suffer those things and that has now suffered them.

Just one more word on the text. Where the Vulgate translates "my blood, which shall be shed for you" (Luke 22:20, Douay-Rheims), the original reads "which is poured out," that is, in the present tense. It is the same when he speaks of the means by which he will be captured and put to death: "Woe to that man by whom the Son of man is betrayed!" (Matt. 26:24). In that case, he speaks in the present tense because his death has already been resolved upon and planned for the following day. In the other, it is so that at the same time that we receive his body and blood, we might regard his death as present.

Christian: you have seen all of the words that bear upon the establishment of this mystery. What simplicity! What precision in these words! He leaves nothing to be interpreted or commented upon. If there is any commentary to be made upon them at all, it is only to remark that according to the force of the original Greek, we ought to render it thus: "This is my body, my very body; the same body that is given for you. This is my blood, my very blood, the blood of the new covenant; the blood poured out for you in remission of your sins." The Greek liturgy puts it this way: "What we are given, what is made of this bread and wine, is the very body of Jesus and his very blood."

There is the commentary we require. What simplicity, what precision, what force do these words have!

If Jesus had wanted to give us a sign, a mere resemblance, he would have known how to tell us. He knew quite well that God had said, when instituting circumcision, "You shall be circumcised in the flesh ... and it shall be a sign of the covenant between me and you" (Gen. 17:11). When he proposed metaphors, he knew quite well how to adapt his language so as to be understood without doubt: "I am the door; if any one enters by me, he will be saved" (John 10:9). "I am the vine, you are the branches. He who abides in me, and I in him, he it is that bears much fruit" (John 15:5). When he made these comparisons and spoke in metaphors, the evangelists said so: "Another parable he put before them" (Matt. 13:24); "he taught them many things in parables" (Mark 4:2). Here, without any introduction, without any qualification, without any explanation, neither before nor after, we are simply told: "Jesus said, 'Take, eat; this is my body; this is my blood'" (Matt. 26:26, 28).

This is what I give to you, and you, what will you do in receiving it? Remember eternally the gift that I gave you that night. Remember that it is I who left it for you and who made this testament, that I left you this Passover, and that I ate it with you before I suffered. If I give you my body as about to be and as having been handed over for you, and my blood as poured out for your sins, in a word, if I give myself to you as a victim, eat it as a victim and remember that this is a promise that it has been sacrificed for you. O my Savior: what simplicity, yet what authority and power there are in your words! "Woman, you are freed from your infirmity" (Luke 13:12); she was healed that instant. "This is my body"; it is his Body. "This is my blood"; it is his Blood. Who can speak in such a manner except the one who holds everything in his hand? Who can make himself be believed except the one to whom to do and to say is the same thing?

My soul, stop here and go no further. Believe as simply, as forcibly as your Savior has spoken, with a submission that corresponds to his authority and power. Once again, he wants to see in your faith the same simplicity with which he has spoken these words. In the ancient rite of Communion, the priest said, "The body of Jesus

Christ," and the faithful responded, "Amen," or "so it is," and "The blood of Jesus Christ," and the faithful responded, "Amen," "so it is." All has been accomplished. All has been said. All has been explained. I am silent. I believe. I adore.

Good Friday

The Passion

Jesus, desiring to enrich us, first gave us his blood to purify us so that we might be able to receive the gifts he offers. O my dear Savior, you go out to the Garden of Olives, to the house of Caiaphas, to the praetorium of the Roman governor, and at last you climb Mount Calvary. Everywhere you go you pour out the blood of your new covenant, the blood by which our crimes are expiated and abolished.

Let us contemplate Jesus in his sorrowful Passion and see the precious blood of the new alliance flow forth, the blood by which we have been redeemed. It first flows in the Garden of Olives. The robes of my Savior are pierced, and the earth is moistened by the bloody sweat of his body. O God! What is this spectacle that so bewilders us? What is, rather, this mystery that both cleanses and sanctifies us?

Is not the answer that our Savior knew that our salvation was in his blood? And that from his ardent desire to save our souls, his blood burst forth, blood which holds within itself our life much more than his own? Thus it seems that this divine blood, so desirous of flowing forth for us, overflowed by the force of his charity, before any violence had been done to him. Let us rush with faith to receive this blood. "O earth, cover not this blood!" (cf. Job 16:18). It is poured out for our souls.

This unprecedented sweat reveals another mystery. In his desire to expiate our crimes, Jesus voluntarily abandoned himself to an infinite sorrow for all of our excesses. He saw them all, one by one, and was afflicted by them beyond measure, as if he himself had committed them, for he was charged with them before God. Yes, our iniquities poured upon him from every direction, so that he could say with David, "the torrents of iniquity troubled me" (Ps. 17:5, Douay-Rheims [RSV = Ps. 18:4]). This is why he said, "Now is my soul troubled" (John 12:27). This was the cause of the inexplicable anguish that brought him to pronounce these words: "My soul is very sorrowful, even to death" (Matt. 26:38). The immensity of sorrow could, in fact, have dealt the death-blow itself, if Jesus had not restrained his soul, preserving it to endure greater evils and to drink the whole cup of his Passion. He nevertheless allowed his blood to overflow in the Garden of Olives to convince us that our sins—yes, our sins alone, without the executioner's help—could have brought about his death. Can you believe that sin could have such great and evil power? If we only saw Jesus fall into the hands of the soldiers who scourged, tormented, and crucified him, we would blame his death only upon this torture. Now that we see him succumb in the Garden of Olives, where he has only our sins to persecute him, we may accuse ourselves. Let us weep, beat our breasts, and tremble in the very depths of our conscience. How could we not be seized with fright, having ourselves, in our very hearts, so certain a cause of death? If sin alone sufficed to kill God, how can mortal men survive with such a poison in their bodies? No. We exist only by a continuous miracle of mercy. The same divine power that miraculously sustained the soul of the Savior, that he might endure the whole punishment, sustains ours that we might accomplish our penance, or at least begin it.

After our Savior had made his blood pour forth by the force of his afflicted charity alone, we can easily believe that he would not spare it from the cruel persecutors of his innocence. Wherever Jesus was during the course of his Passion, a furious cruelty wounded him again and again. If we were to accompany him to each of the places he went, we would see the bloody tracks that marked his way. The chief priest's house, the Roman judge's tribunal, the guard house where Jesus was handed over to the brutal insolence of the soldiers, and all the streets of Jerusalem are stained with the divine blood that purified Heaven and earth.

We should never come to an end should we attempt to consider all of the cruel circumstances in which this innocent blood was shed. It suffices to say that on this day of blood and carnage, on this day at once deadly and salvific, on which the powers of Hell were loosed upon Jesus Christ, he renounced his own power. While his enemies were able to do all that they wished, he voluntarily reduced himself to the condition of enduring all. By the effect of the same divine plan, God loosened the bridle of the envious and held back all the power of his Son. While all the powers of Hell were unchained, the protection of Heaven was withdrawn, so that Jesus was exposed naked and disarmed, powerless and without being able to resist, to anyone who wished to insult him.

After this, need we contemplate the infinite details of his sorrow? Need we consider how he was ruthlessly handed over to lackeys and soldiers to be the object of their bloody scorn and to suffer from their insolence every blow that their pitiless mockery and malicious cruelty could deal? Need we imagine this dear Savior allowing his body to feel the strength of these executioners, their hard scourge upon his back, the sharp spines upon his head? O divine Jesus! How much blood did it cost the God-man to win our salvation!

The new covenant was not yet sealed, for his veins had not yet been emptied upon the Cross. We must consider the sufferings of a man whose limbs are bruised and broken by a violent hanging, no longer even feeling his wounds, hanging from hands torn by the weight of his body, completely beaten by the loss of his blood. Amid this excessive pain, he was lifted up, it seemed, for the sole purpose of seeing the crowd of people mock him and laugh at his deplorable condition. After all this, could we be surprised if Jesus were to ask, "Is there any sorrow like my sorrow?" (cf. Lam. 1:12).

Our hearts should be made tender by this pitiable sight. We must not leave the great spectacle of Calvary with dry eyes. There is no heart so hardened that it can see human blood spilled and not be moved. But the blood of Jesus gives our hearts the grace of compunction, which is the emotion of penitence. Those who remained near his Cross and watched him breathe his final breath, "returned home beating their breasts" (Luke 23:48). Jesus Christ, dying a cruel death and spilling his innocent blood, poured out a spirit of compunction and penitence upon the whole of Mount Calvary. We must not let our hearts be hardened. Let us make Calvary echo with the sound of our sobbing. Let us weep bitter tears for our sins and turn against ourselves with a holy anger. Let us break all our unworthy habits and leave behind our worldly lives. Let us carry in ourselves the death of Jesus Christ.

Holy Saturday

The Brevity of Life

Like every finite thing, man is small. The time will come when this man who seemed so great to us will cease to be. The days of my life are all that stand between me and nothingness, and this is but a small difference. I enter into life under a law that commands my departure from it. I come to make my mark and to show myself as others do. Afterward, I will disappear. I have seen others pass before me; others shall succeed me, and these will present the same spectacle to their successors. All of us will at last be mixed together in nothingness.

My life, all told, has been only a handful of years; and there were so many before me and will be so many after. How small a place do I occupy in the great abyss of time! I am nothing. This short interval is not capable of distinguishing me from the nothingness into which I must return. I have come only to take my number, and to this point no use has been made of me. The drama would have been no worse acted had I remained offstage. My part in this world is very small, and so insignificant that it seems to me only a dream that I am here, and all that I see an empty image: "the form of this world is passing away" (1 Cor. 7:31).

The whole of my career has been only a handful of years; and in reaching this age how many perils have I escaped? How many illnesses? What has kept the course of my days from having come to an end at any moment? Death prepares many ambushes. In the end, we will fall into its hands. I see a tree battered by the wind; it loses leaves every minute; some resist more, others less; but those few that escape the storm will at last be conquered by winter, which always comes to wither them and make them fall. It is the same in life. The large number of men who run the same course ensures that some of them will reach the end of it; but after having avoided the various attacks of death, and arriving at the end after so many perils, they fall at the race's end. Their life extinguishes itself like a candle that consumes its own matter.

My life has been only a handful of years, and of these, in how many of them have I really lived? Sleep resembles death more than life; childhood is the life of a beast. How many days would I like to erase from the days of my youth? And when I am older, how many more shall I add to that total? Let us see what remains. What shall I then count, if all of these are not to be reckoned? The time during which I felt a certain contentment, or in which I acquired some honor? But how much of this sort of time is scattered throughout my life? If I take away sleep, illnesses, and times of anxiety from my life, and I now take up all of the things in which I have had some contentment or honor, how much will that be? As to this contentment: did I enjoy it all at once? Have I not had it in parcels? Have I had it without anxiety? And, if there has been anxiety, should I count it as time that I reckon or time that I do not? Has not anxiety always divided every two moments of contentment? Is it not always thrown across them to prevent them from meeting one another? What then is left to me? Of lawful pleasures, a useless memory; of illicit ones, regret, and a debt to be paid in Hell, or by penance.

How right we are to say that our time passes! Truly it passes, and we pass with it. My whole being rests upon a single moment: it is all that separates me from nothingness. When that moment has passed, I snatch another one. They pass one after the other, and one after the other I join them together, trying to reassure myself, and I do not perceive that they carry me with them, and that I will soon be out of time. This is my life, and what is so frightening is that what to my sight seems fleeting is to God an eternal present. These things have to do with me. What belongs to me belongs to time, because I myself depend upon time. Yet they belong to God before they belong to me, and they depend upon God before they depend upon time. Time cannot wrest them from his empire, for he is above time. To him, they remain, and they enter among his treasures. What I have lost I will find again. What I do in time passes through time to eternity, for time is comprehended by and is under the rule of eternity and leads to eternity. I enjoy the moments of this life only as they pass; when they pass, I must respond to them as if they had remained. It is not enough to say, "They have gone, I will think no more of them." They are gone to me, yes, but to God, no, and he will ask me for a reckoning of them.

If this life is a small thing because it is passing, what are we to think of those pleasures that do not last for a whole lifetime and which pass by in a moment? Are they worth their price? O my God, I resolve with all my heart, in your presence, every day, to think about death, at least when I lie down and when I rise. And with this thought: "I have little time, I have a long road to travel, perhaps I have less further to go than I think." I will praise God for having brought me to think about repentance, and I will put order into my affairs, into my confession, into my meditation, thinking not about what passes, but with great care, great courage, and great diligence about what remains.

Moses and Jesus Christ

God allowed Moses to be thrown into the Nile and then delivered him to show the chosen people that he was their liberator (Exod. 2:3). Thus, like Jonah, Moses prefigured Christ, whose Resurrection neither the tomb nor its horrors could impede.

When Moses "had grown up," God inspired him to leave the court of Pharaoh and the princess his daughter, who had raised him as her own child, and go "out to his people" (Exod. 2:11). This is explained by St. Paul: "Moses, when he was grown up, refused to be called the son of Pharaoh's daughter, choosing rather to share ill-treatment with the people of God than to enjoy the fleeting pleasures of sin. He considered abuse suffered for the Christ greater wealth than the treasures of Egypt … by faith he left Egypt, not being afraid of the anger of the king," who henceforth sought his death (Heb. 11:24-27). He took up the defense of the Israelites by a divine instinct, avenging them upon an Egyptian who had mistreated them, and, as St. Stephen says, "He supposed that his brethren understood that God was giving them deliverance by his hand, but they did not understand" (Acts 7:25). For Moses to save them, it was necessary that he suffer their opposition, which was so pronounced that he was forced to take flight. And so persecution came from those he was to save, and by this means God showed him to be like their Savior, an image of Jesus Christ.

"And the Lord said to Moses, 'See, I make you as God to Pharaoh; and Aaron your brother shall be your prophet'" (Exod. 7:1). The savior of the holy people had to be like God. Elsewhere the Lord says, "You are gods, sons of the Most High" (Ps. 82:6); here he says, "I make you *as* God." It is a mark of divinity to have prophets, which is why they are called the prophets of the Lord; here God tells Moses that Aaron "shall be *your* prophet." Moses is robed with God's omnipotence. He has thunder in his hand, in the form of the rod that strikes rivers and changes water into blood, strikes again and makes them return to their nature, and is raised to the heavens to call forth a deep darkness, but which, like God himself, he separates from the light, for the people of Israel remain in the light while the Egyptians are enveloped in a dark cloud and are unable to move. This powerful rod makes frogs and grasshoppers come forth from the earth, changes the dust into flies, sends an inexorable plague upon all the animals of Egypt, and effects the other prodigies that are written in the book of Exodus.

Here, then, we see Moses like a God, accomplishing all that he wills both in the heavens and on the earth and holding all nature under his power. It is true that God places a limit upon the power he gives to Moses: "I make you as God to Pharaoh." It was not thus with the Savior of the new people, who is called God absolutely, because "all things were made through him" (John 1:3), and whom St. Paul calls "God over all, blessed for ever" (Rom. 9:5). For the servant must not equal the master. "Moses was faithful in all God's house as a servant … but Christ was faithful over God's house as a son" (Heb. 3:5-6).

Through Moses, God established an everlasting monument to the deliverance of his people: the ceremony of the Passover. He would send his angel to bring death and mourning to every Egyptian family, by smiting "all the first-born in the land of Egypt, from the first-born of Pharaoh who sat on his throne to the first-born of the captive who was in the dungeon, and all the first-born of the cattle" (cf. Exod. 12:29). After this last plague, and fearing total devastation, the Egyptians "were urgent with the people, to send them out of the land in haste" (Exod. 12:33). While the avenging angel wrought the desolation of the Egyptians, the Israelites were preserved by the blood of the Paschal lamb. Take a lamb "without blemish," that is, a perfect image of Jesus (Exod. 12:5). Like Jesus, this lamb must be slain and eaten. "Take a bunch of hyssop," Moses told the elders, "and dip it in the blood" of the lamb, and "touch the lintel and the two doorposts with the blood … for the Lord will pass through to slay the Egyptians; and when he sees the blood on the lintel and on the doorposts, the Lord will pass over the door, and will not allow the destroyer to enter your houses to slay you" (Exod. 12:22-23). God did not need the sensible sign in order to distinguish between his holy people and the victims of his anger. The sign was for us. He wanted to show us that the blood of the true spotless lamb would be the sacred character by which God would separate the children of Egypt—to whom God would bring death—and the children of Israel, whose lives he would save.

Let us, with St. Paul, carry in our bodies "the death of Jesus" (2 Cor. 4:10), the mark of his blood, if we wish to be spared from the divine anger. Everything about the Paschal lamb is a prophetic mystery. Its bones were not to be broken, for the bones of Jesus were spared even though the bones of the men crucified with him were broken. The lamb was to be eaten in traveler's garb, by those ready to depart at the merest word, and this is the posture and condition of the disciple of Jesus, of those who eat his flesh and are nourished by his substance, whose life is both according to the body and to the spirit. "You shall eat it in haste" (Exod. 12:11). There should be nothing slow or indolent in those who are nourished with the food that Jesus has given us. The whole lamb was to be eaten: head, feet, and entrails. Not only are the most noble and the most intimate parts of Jesus worthy, but so are the most humble. For even what was lowliest in him—his suffering, his sadness, the troubles of his holy soul, his sweat of blood, his agony—was for the sake of our salvation and to provide an example for us. Have no doubt about his weaknesses. Do not blush for his humiliation. A firm and lively faith will devour it all. And seek not sensible pleasure, for this lamb was to be eaten with bitter herbs, with distaste for the world and its pleasures, and, should God will it, without even the sensible taste of devotion, for ours remains impure and carnal. Such is the mystery of the Paschal lamb.

Yet if there was in Moses, the savior of the holy people, so manifest a ray of divinity and so exalted a participation in the title of God, should we be surprised if the substance and the "whole fullness of deity dwells bodily" in Jesus Christ (Col. 2:9), who, in saving us from sin saves us from every evil? To complete the prefigurement, Moses was both "as God to Pharaoh" and at the same time the mediator. Pharaoh said to him: "Entreat the Lord" (Exod. 8:8). And at the prayer of Moses, God turned aside his scourges and brought the plagues to an end. Thus Jesus, who is our God, is at the same time our mediator (1 Tim. 2:5), our all-powerful intercessor, to whom God refuses nothing, and "there is no other name under heaven given among men by which we must be saved" (Acts 4:12).

Let us place all our confidence in Jesus, the Paschal lamb, at once God and mediator. Moses was "as God to Pharaoh" only to bring plagues, and he was a mediator only to send them away. But Jesus "went about doing good and healing all that were oppressed" (Acts 10:38). He made use of his power only to show forth his goodness, and the plagues from which he freed us are the plagues of the spirit. Let us place ourselves in his life-giving hands. He asks for nothing more than that we give ourselves to him. Then he will save us, for "salvation is from the Lord" (Ps. 3:9, Douay-Rheims).

Easter

To Unite Ourselves with Christ

At the end of these meditations, I ask you to rise up above not only all that I have said, which is nothing, but even all that man can say, and to listen only to what God says to you in the heart and to unite yourself to it in faith. For this is truly what it means to pray with Jesus Christ and in Jesus Christ: to be united in spirit with the prayer of Christ himself. Being thus united to Jesus Christ, God and man, and through him to God the Father, we also unite ourselves in him to all the faithful and with all mankind.

To accomplish this work of unity, we should no longer see the world except in Christ. We ought to believe that every single ray of faith that is in us is a mere spark of the love that the eternal Father has for his Son, and because the Son our Savior is in us, the Father's love extends to us as well. It was unto this end that Jesus prayed.

The Church, always praying through our Lord Jesus Christ, is thereby united to the prayer of Christ himself.

If the Church celebrates the grace and glory of the holy Apostles, the shepherds of the flock, she acknowledges that their grace and glory come from Christ's prayer for them. The saints joined together in glory were no less included in the view and the intention of Christ, even though he did not say so expressly. Who can doubt that he saw all those his Father was to give him through the centuries to come and for whom he was going to die with particular and great affection?

Let us then enter with Jesus and in Jesus into the building up of the whole body of the Church, and giving thanks with her through Jesus Christ for all the saints in glory, let us ask for the salvation of the whole body of Christ, the whole society of the saints. Let us ask with confidence that we will find ourselves counted among the blessed, doubting not that this gift will be given to us if we persevere in asking for mercy and grace, that is, by the merit of the blood that was poured out for us, the sacred promise of which we have in the Eucharist.

After this prayer, let us go with Jesus to the sacrifice. Together with him let us go up the two holy mountains, the Mount of Olives and Mount Calvary, and, with him, let us pass from one to the other: from the Mount of Olives, the mount of agony, to Mount Calvary, the mount of death; from the Mount of Olives, where battle is joined, to Mount Calvary, where victory is won; from the Mount of Olives, the mountain of resignation, to Mount Calvary, the mountain of sacrifice; from the one where he said, "Not my will, but thine be done" (Luke 22:42), to the one where he said, "Father, into thy hands I commit my spirit" (Luke 23:46). And in sum, from the mountain on which we prepare ourselves for every sacrifice, to the one on which we die to the world with Jesus Christ, to whom be given all honor and glory, with the Father, and the Holy Spirit, world without end. Amen.

Solemnity of Saint Joseph

A Man after His Own Heart

The man whose heart is in accord with God's makes no display, nor does God choose him for his appearance or by listening to the voice of the people. When Samuel was sent to the house of Jesse to find David—the first to have merited such praise—the great man destined by God for the world's most glorious throne was not known even to his family. He was not thought of while his older brothers were being brought before the prophet. Yet God, who does not judge as man does, secretly warned Samuel not to regard their great stature or hardy countenance. And so, rejecting those who had been put forward in the world, he bid to approach the one who had been sent to watch the sheep, and pouring the oil of royalty upon his head, he left his parents astonished to have so little known the son chosen by God for such an extraordinary advantage.

A similar design of Divine Providence allows us to apply what was said of David to Joseph, the son of David.

A Man after His Own Heart

The time had come when God sought a man after his own heart in order to place in his hands what was dearest to him: the person of his only-begotten Son, the integrity of his holy mother, the salvation of mankind, the treasure of heaven and earth. He overlooks Jerusalem and the other famous towns and rests his gaze upon Nazareth, and from this unknown hamlet chooses an unknown man, a poor craftsman, Joseph, and entrusts to him a work that would not bring shame to the highest order of angels, so that we might understand that the man after God's own heart must be sought in the heart and is made worthy by his hidden virtues.

Christian justice is a private affair between a man and God: it is a mystery between them that is profaned when it is revealed, and which cannot be too carefully hidden from those who are not privy to the secret. This is why the Son of God enjoins us to retire by ourselves and to pray with the door shut. The Christian life should be a hidden life, and the true Christian should ardently desire to remain hidden under God's wing without having any other spectator.

Yet here nature cries out, for it cannot abide this obscurity; nature recoils from death, and to live hidden and unknown is to be dead in the minds of men. Life is found in activity, and the one who ceases to act seems also to have ceased to live. Men of the world who are accustomed to tumult and hurry do not know what peaceable, interior activity is; they do not think themselves to be doing anything unless they are anxious, and therefore they consider retreat and obscurity to be a kind of death. They understand life to be found in the world, and so they persuade themselves that they are not entirely dead as long as their name finds some echo upon the earth. This is why reputation seems to them to be a second life: to survive in the memory of men is a distinction they hold in great account. It takes little to make them believe that they will secretly come out of their tombs to hear what will be said about them, so strongly persuaded are they that to live is to make some noise and to stir up the affairs of men. Here is the eternity promised by the world, an eternity in titles, immortality by renown. It is a vain and fragile immortality, but one made much of by the conquerors of old. It is this false imagination that makes obscurity seem a kind of death to those who love the world, and even something worse than death, for, in their opinion, to live hidden and unknown is to be buried alive.

Our Lord Jesus Christ, having come to die and to sacrifice himself, wished to do so completely: and so he was not content to die a natural death, nor the most cruel and violent death, but he wished to add to that a civic and political death. And as this civic death came by two means, both by infamy and by being forgotten, he wished to suffer both of them. A victim of human pride, he wished to sacrifice himself by all sorts of humiliations, and he gave his first thirty years to that death of being forgotten. To die with Jesus Christ, we must die this death, so that we might say with St. Paul: "The world has been crucified to me, and I to the world" (Gal. 6:14).

The world is dead to us when we leave it. But this is not enough; in order to arrive at perfection we must be dead to it and it must leave us, that is to say that we should place ourselves in such a condition that we no longer please the world, that it holds us for dead, and that it no longer takes us to belong to its parties and intrigues, nor even to its conversations. This is the high perfection of Christianity, and it is here that one finds life, because here one learns to enjoy God, who does not live in the whirlwind or in the tumult of the world, but in the peace and solitude of retirement.

Joseph was dead in this way. He was buried with Jesus Christ and the Blessed Virgin, and he was not at all troubled by a death which enabled him to live with his Savior. On the contrary, he feared nothing more than that the noise and the life of the world would come to disturb his hidden and interior repose. It is an admirable mystery:

Joseph had in his house what could have attracted the eyes of the whole world, and the world did not know it. He possessed a God-man, and he said not one word about it; he is the witness of so great a mystery, and he enjoyed it in secret, without divulging it! The Magi and the shepherds came to adore Jesus Christ; Simeon and Anna publicized his greatness; no other could have given better testimony of the mystery of Jesus Christ than the one who was its custodian, who knew the miracle of his birth, and whom the angel had so well instructed. What father would not speak about so admirable a son?

And despite the ardor of so many holy souls who would have sat before him with great zeal to celebrate the praise of Jesus Christ, he was not able to open his mouth to tell them the secret that God had confided to him. *Erant mirantes*, said the evangelist (Luke 2:33): they seemed astonished, it was as though they knew nothing. They heard all the others speak, and they kept so religiously silent that it was still said of him after thirty years in the village "Is this not the son of Joseph?" (cf. John 6:42) without any of them having learned of the mystery of his virginal conception.

It is because Mary and Joseph knew that in order to enjoy God in truth, one must retire with God and be content to see him alone.

A Man after His Own Heart

Where shall we find spiritual and interior men in an age when brilliance is everything? When I consider men in their work, their business, their activities, I find confirmation of St. John Chrysostom's dictum that all our actions have only human ends in view. For how many shall we find who do not turn aside from the straight and narrow when they find their path blocked by powerful obstacles, or who do not seek an accord between what justice requires and what popularity asks of them, between duty and the desire to please? How many shall we find to whom the prejudice of opinion, the tyranny of custom, the fear of shocking the world does not cause to seek some middle ground between Jesus Christ and Belial, between the gospel and the age? If there are, indeed, some whose virtuous desires are not entirely smothered by human respect, how many of these are content to await their crown until the next life and who do not want to earn some of the fruit in advance in the form of human praise? This is the plague of Christian virtue.

Virtue is like a plant that can die in two ways: by being ripped out or by being allowed to dry up. A torrent of water uproots it and casts it upon the soil; a dry spell withers it upon its stalk. It is the same with virtue. You love equity and justice, but some great interest is presented to you, or some violent passion makes your love of justice rise impetuously in your heart: if you allow yourself to be carried off by the storm, a torrent of water uproots your soul. You languish for a time under the trial of your weakness, but in the end you allow passion to carry off your heart. The whole world is amazed to see that you have lost the virtue that you had so carefully cultivated.

Yet when these violent efforts have been resisted, do not think that you have been saved. You must beware of the other danger, the danger of praise. The opposing vice uproots virtue, but the love of praise causes it to wither. It seems to hold its position well, to stand firm, but it deceives the eyes of men. The root is withered; it draws no more nourishment; it is good only to be cast in the fire. It is the dry grass of the rooftops of which David spoke, "that dries itself out before it is pulled forth" (cf. Ps. 129:6). How desirable it is not to have been born in a high place, but instead to live in some deserted valley! How devoutly we should wish that our virtue will not be exposed in a lofty place, but instead be nourished by Christian humility in some forgotten corner!

Joseph merited the greatest honors because he was never touched by honor. The Church has nothing more illustrious, because it has nothing more hidden. May the Almighty God ensure that we shall always revere Joseph's hidden virtue.

The Handmaiden

The holy Fathers say with one accord that the principle of our ruin was pride, and the reason for this is plain: from the sacred Scriptures we learn that the fall of man was prompted by Satan. This proud spirit fell upon us. Like a large building that falls over and crushes a smaller one beneath it, so did this proud spirit topple over onto us and envelop us in his ruin. By falling upon us, he impressed upon us a movement similar to his own. Having been beaten by his own pride, he pulled us after him, so that we are now as proud as he, and this pride is our most deadly vice.

Of all the vices, it is the one that is most opposed to its remedy and which most greatly separates us from mercy. For man, wretched as he is, would be easily rendered worthy of pity if he had not been proud. It is easy enough to have compassion for unhappy people who submit themselves, but, as St. Augustine says, "There is

no one more unworthy of compassion than a proud suf-
ferer, one who joins arrogance to weakness." This is the
condition in which we were: at once weak and haughty,
powerless and yet bold. This presumption closed the door
on mercy; therefore, in order to relieve our misery it was
first necessary to cure us of our pride. To attract compassion, we first had to learn humility. This is the reason
God humbled himself in the womb of the Blessed Virgin
and took upon himself the form of a slave.

Here we ought to admire the method God employed
to cure human arrogance, and to do this it is necessary to
explain the nature of our stubborn illness. Pride, as St.
Augustine tells us, is a false and pernicious imitation of
God's greatness: "Those who rise up against you," he says,
addressing God, "imitate you in a disordered way." This
account makes good sense, but a nice distinction made
by the same Father will help us to see farther. There are
some things that God allows us to imitate, and others he
does not. What excites his jealousy is when man wants to
make himself God and resemble him, but not every kind
of resemblance is offensive.

For he has made us in his image, and we carry upon
ourselves the impression of his countenance and the mark
of his perfections. There are divine attributes which our
attempts to resemble do not make him angry with us; on

the contrary, he commands it. For instance, consider his mercy, of which it is said in the Scriptures that it "is over all that he has made" (Ps. 145:9). He has ordained us to conform to this model: "Be merciful, even as your Father is merciful" (Luke 6:36). God is patient with sinners, inviting them to repentance, and while he waits for them to return, he causes the sun to shine on them. He wants us to show ourselves to be his children by imitating this patience with regard to our enemies, "so that you may be sons of your Father who is in heaven" (Matt. 5:45). Likewise, as he is truthful, we can imitate him in his truthfulness. He is just; we can follow him in his justice. He is holy, and even though his holiness seems entirely incommunicable, he is nevertheless not angered if we dare to resemble him in this marvelous attribute. On the contrary, he commands it: "You shall be holy; for I the Lord your God am holy" (Lev. 19:2).

What is the resemblance that makes him so jealous? It is when we wish to resemble his independence by taking our will as its own sovereign law, just as he himself has no law beyond his absolute will. This is where he is touchy; this is his point of delicacy. This is when he violently pushes back those who would injure the majesty of his empire. Let us be gods: he allows it through the imitation of his holiness, justice, patience, and ever-generous mercy. But as to his power, let us keep ourselves within the bounds proper to a creature, and not allow our desires to extend to so dangerous a resemblance.

Here is the unchanging rule that distinguishes between what we can and what we cannot imitate in God. But oh, how depraved are the sons of Adam! Oh, how strange is the corruption of our hearts! We reverse this beautiful order. We do not wish to imitate him in the things in which he proposes himself to us as a model, and in those in which he wishes to be unique and inimitable, we attempt to counterfeit him. For if we were to imitate him in his holiness, would the prophet say, "Help, Lord; for there is no longer any one that is godly" (Ps. 12:1)? Or if we were to imitate his fidelity or his justice, would the prophet Micah say: "The godly man has perished from the earth, and there is none upright among men; they all lie in wait for blood, and each hunts his brother with a net" (Micah 7:2)? And so we do not wish to imitate God in these excellent traits whose living image is so easy to see in us. Instead that sovereignty, that independence which we are not allowed to grasp: these we seek. This is the sacred and inviolable right that we dare to usurp.

For, as St. Augustine explains, just as God has no one above him who rules and governs him, so also do we wish to be the arbiters of our conduct, so that by casting off the yoke, cutting the reins, and spitting out the bridle of the commandment that restrains our wayward liberty, we might depend upon no other power and be as gods upon the earth. This false estimation of our independence makes us irritable in the face of laws. The one who prohibits us incites us, as if we were to say in our hearts: "What! Someone dares to command me!" We take offense at laws as we would at some great injury done to our person.

Is this not what God himself holds against the proud, under the image of the prince of Tyre: "Because your heart is proud, and you have said, 'I am a god, I sit in the seat of gods'" (Ezek. 28:2). You wanted neither to be ruled by nor to depend upon another. You are full of yourself, and you ascribe all things to yourself. When you have seen your fortune founded by your skill and intrigue, you did not remember the hand of God, and you said with Pharaoh "My Nile is my own," that is, this whole great domain belongs to me, it is the fruit of my labor, "I made it" (Ezek. 29:3).

Thus does our blind pride set us up as petty gods. Well then, O proud man, O little god: behold the great living God who lowers himself to confound you. Man has made himself god through his pride. God makes himself man through his humility. Man falsely credits himself with

God's greatness, and God truly takes on man's nothingness. For thus we should consider what happens today in the blessed womb of the holy Virgin. There, God empties and annihilates himself by taking the form of a slave so that the slave might be confounded when he wishes to make himself the master and lord.

Here is a new secret of the divine mercy, which wished not only to confound our pride, but even to condescend to the point of giving it a certain kind of satisfaction. For it was necessary to give something to this unruly passion, which will never entirely surrender. Man had dared to aspire to the divine independence. He could not be contented on this point: the throne cannot be divided and the sovereign Majesty cannot suffer an equal. Yet here is a counsel of mercy that will be capable of satisfying our pride: if we cannot resemble God in his sovereign independence, he wishes to resemble us in our humility. Man can never become independent. In order to satisfy him, God becomes submissive. His sovereign grandeur will not allow itself to be abased while remaining in himself, but this infinitely abundant nature does not refuse to go borrowing in order to enrich itself by humility, so that, as St. Augustine says, "the man who disdains humility, who calls it simplicity and baseness when he sees it in other men, will not disdain to practice it, seeing it in God."

Such is God's plan to cure human arrogance: he chose to rip out of our hearts that indomitable pride that submits only with disdain and dominates with glee, which cannot abide any burden or law, even those given by God. This is why there is no lowliness or servitude to which Christ does not descend: he abandoned himself to the will of his Father.

Let us carefully weigh these words: he took the form of a slave. He took upon himself the human nature that obliged him to be a subject, he who was born king. He descends still further. He took the form of a slave because he appeared like a sinner, because he himself was robed with "the likeness of sinful flesh" (Rom. 8:3), and in this way he bore the marks of a slave, such as circumcision, and he lived a servile life: "the Son of man came not to be served but to serve" (Matt. 20:28). He abased himself much further. He took the form of a slave because he was not only similar to sinners, but he was the public victim for all sinners. From the first moment of his conception — "when Christ came into the world," as the apostle said — he took upon himself the condition of victim, and he said, "Lo, I have come to do thy will, O God" (Heb. 10:5, 7).

Lest we think that in submitting himself to the will of God he exempted himself from depending upon the will of men, let us recall that he was handed over as a victim to the will of sinful men, to the will of Hell: "But this is your hour," he said, "and the power of darkness" (Luke 22:53). He did not await the Cross to make this submission. Mary was the first altar upon which he was immolated. Mary was the temple where he first rendered homage to God, where for the first time this great and marvelous spectacle of a God submissive and obedient even unto death, even giving himself up for sinners and to Hell itself in order that they might have their way with him. Why this abasement? To confound our pride.

In the sight of so profound an abasement, who could refuse to submit? Of what obedience can we complain when we see the wills of the men to whom the Savior of souls submitted? To the will of the cowardly Pilate, of the treasonous Judas, of the High Priests, and of the barbaric soldiers who made sport of him? After this example of submission, we ought to cherish the lowest places, which, after the abasement of the incarnate God, have henceforth become the most honorable.

Mary joins us today in these sentiments. Even though her angelic purity was a powerful attraction to make Jesus Christ be born in her, it was not her purity that brought this mystery to its consummation: it was her humility and her obedience. If Mary had not said that she was a

The Handmaiden

handmaiden, in vain would she have been a virgin, and we would not exclaim today that her womb is blessed. Let us profit from this lesson. Let us meditate attentively upon this truth.

Sophia Institute

Sophia Institute is a nonprofit institution that seeks to nurture the spiritual, moral, and cultural life of souls and to spread the Gospel of Christ in conformity with the authentic teachings of the Roman Catholic Church.

Sophia Institute Press fulfills this mission by offering translations, reprints, and new publications that afford readers a rich source of the enduring wisdom of mankind.

Sophia Institute also operates two popular online Catholic resources: CrisisMagazine.com and CatholicExchange.com.

Crisis Magazine provides insightful cultural analysis that arms readers with the arguments necessary for navigating the ideological and theological minefields of the day. *Catholic Exchange* provides world news from a Catholic perspective as well as daily devotionals and articles that will help you to grow in holiness and live a life consistent with the teachings of the Church.

In 2013, Sophia Institute launched Sophia Institute for Teachers to renew and rebuild Catholic culture through service to Catholic education. With the goal of nurturing the spiritual, moral, and cultural life of souls, and an abiding respect for the role and work of teachers, we strive to provide materials and programs that are at once enlightening to the mind and ennobling to the heart; faithful and complete, as well as useful and practical.

Sophia Institute gratefully recognizes the Solidarity Association for preserving and encouraging the growth of our apostolate over the course of many years. Without their generous and timely support, this book would not be in your hands.

www.SophiaInstitute.com
www.CatholicExchange.com
www.CrisisMagazine.com
www.SophiaInstituteforTeachers.org

Sophia Institute Press® is a registered trademark of Sophia Institute.
Sophia Institute is a tax-exempt institution as defined by the Internal Revenue Code, Section 501(c)(3). Tax I.D. 22-2548708.